Conceptualism and Other Fictions
The Collected Writings of Eduardo Costa
1965–2015

Edited by Patrick Greaney

Work published within the framework of the "Sur" Translation Support Program of the Ministry of Foreign Affairs, International Trade and Worship of the Argentine Republic.

Obra editada en el marco del Programa "Sur" de Apoyo a las Traducciones del Ministerio de Relaciones Exteriores, Comercio Internacional y Culto de la República Argentina.

Conceptualism and Other Fictions: Collected Writings of Eduardo Costa 1965–2015 ©2016
Eduardo Costa

Conceptualism and Other Fictions: Collected Writings of Eduardo Costa 1965–2015
FIRST EDITION

Edited by Patrick Greaney
Translations by Jen Hofer and John Pluecker

Text and cover design by Les Figues Press.

ISBN 13: 978-1-934254-63-9
ISBN 10:1-934254-63-0
Library of Congress Control Number: 2015954879

Work published within the framework of the "Sur" Translation Support Program of the
Ministry of Foreign Affairs, International Trade and Worship of the Argentine Republic.

Obra editada en el marco del Programa "Sur" de Apoyo a las Traducciones del Ministerio de
Relaciones Exteriores, Comercio Internacional y Culto de la República Argentina.

Les Figues Press thanks its subscribers for their support and readership.
Les Figues Press is a 501c3 organization. Donations are tax-deductible.

Les Figues would like to acknowledge the following individuals for their generosity:
Peter Binkow and Johanna Blakley, Lauren Bon, Elena Karina Byrne, Pam Ore and Sara
LaBorde, Coco Owen, and Dr. Robert Wessels.

Special thanks to: M. Carson Day and Evan Kleekamp.

Les Figues Press titles are available through:
Les Figues Press, http://www.lesfigues.com
Small Press Distribution, http://www.spdbooks.org

IN OTHER WORDS, Book No. 2

Post Office Box 7736
Los Angeles, CA 90007
info@lesfigues.com
www.lesfigues.com

Contents

A Creator of Genres

Conceptualism and Other Fictions: The Collected Writings of Eduardo Costa brings together essays, letters, reviews, scripts, and other texts written in Spanish and English over the past fifty-five years. It's hard to summarize this heterogeneous body of writings, but it's possible to see how, in many of them, Costa focuses on a few areas of interest that are at the heart of his work as an artist: the constitution of codes and systems, the materiality of the artwork, and the relation of art and everyday life.

Since the late 1990s, Costa's originality and historical importance have been widely recognized in the English-speaking world. Exhibitions like *Global Conceptualism* (1999) and *International Pop* (2015) have emphasized his role in those movements. And the first text in Alexander Alberro and Blake Stimson's *Conceptual Art: A Critical Anthology* is a 1966 manifesto co-written by Costa and two other artists. *Conceptualism and Other Fictions* fills in the background for the individual works and texts that appear in those and other exhibitions and anthologies.[1] But the present collection also shows how Costa's works resist inclusion in existing art historical accounts. More than a contributor to any movement, Costa is a "creator of genres."[2] Fashion fictions, street works, tape poems, talking paintings, volumetric paintings: these are just a few of the art forms that he has created or helped create over the past half century. This book touches on many of those genres, but not all of them. These are Costa's "collected writings," but not his "complete writings" or an exhaustive account of his work as an artist.

One of the first examples of a new genre in Costa's corpus is mass media art. In July 1966, a collective made up of Costa, Raúl Escari, and Roberto Jacoby informed the press about a happening, which, in fact, never took place. The three artists knew what the media expected of a happening, and they provided information that met those expectations: explanations of the event's premises along with photos of celebrities participating in the happening.[3] Later, they notified the press that there had been no such happening. "Thus the possibility of a new genre is opened up," they wrote in their manifesto. They called it a "mass media art" in which what matters is not "'what is said' but rather *the thematization of the media as media*."[4] Mass media art focuses attention on the mechanisms of the media that usually remain implicit in the dissemination of information—and makes them into a new kind of aesthetic material.

A few months later, in December 1966, Costa participated in the creation of another genre. Along with four other artists and the critic Oscar Masotta, he organized an event called *On Happenings*. They reenacted happenings by Michael Kirby, Claes Oldenburg, and Carolee Schneemann that they had read about or that Masotta had seen in New York earlier that year. Their "intention," Costa and Masotta write in the essay "On Happenings, Happening: Reflections and an Account," "was not to repeat happenings, but rather to produce, for the audience, a situation that resembled that experienced by archaeologists and psychoanalysts." They thought that their work "would function as a commentary on the history of the happening."[5] As the art historians Ana Longoni and Mariano Mestman write, "It was not events that would be performed, but rather signs of absent, past facts."[6] *On Happenings* used a code that had become historical. Where other artists might have tried to figure out how to best activate that code and create new happenings, Costa and his peers wanted to make the code perceptible and, by reflecting on it, move beyond it to create a new kind of work.

Costa already signaled his interest in decoding operations in the epigraph to his 1965 story "Mental Relations," where he quotes an interview in which Barthes claims that fashion and literature's "being is in signification"—that is, in the processes and codes that make them up—and "not in what is signified."[7] Costa and other Argentine artists mined texts by thinkers like Roland Barthes and Marshall McLuhan for methods that would be fruitful for art, much like the surrealists did with Freud and psychoanalysis.[8] "By writing a poem I say certain things," Barthes writes in a 1960 article on fashion, "but *at the same time* I point to poetry."[9] A similar structure appears in mass media art and *On Happenings*: they point to the media and to the Happening.

In the decades since these first projects, Costa has focused his decoding attention on many things as he has moved between New York, Rio de Janeiro, and Buenos Aires. One of them is the fashion media. In his ongoing *Fashion Fictions*, a series begun in 1966, he had objects made that looked like jewelry (including ears, toes, and strands of hair, all in 24k gold), but that weren't actually meant to be worn. Instead, they functioned as props intended to trigger a reaction in the fashion media. It worked: first in Argentina, where it was covered in the press in 1966 or 1967, and, later, in the United States, where Richard Avedon photographed the model Marisa Berenson wearing one of Costa's creations for the March 1968 edition of *Vogue* and where the photographer Hiro's images of the same object appeared on the cover of *Harper's Bazaar* in October 1968.[10]

Costa's *Fashion Fictions* and his collaborative media art projects are about the media that present them, and, in this way, they are similar to conceptual art, which they anticipated or emerged simultaneously with. Specifically, they are like that kind of conceptual art that thematizes the art apparatus, the "conventions that…frame it or situate it."[11] But his *Fashion Fictions* are not "'conceptual' in the stupid sense of the frequently boring things done with words," as Costa puts it delicately in an interview.[12] His distance from that kind of conceptualism can be seen most clearly in a work that might seem closest to it, since the work consists of just these words typed on a piece of paper: "A piece that is essentially the same as a piece made by any of the first conceptual artists, dated two years earlier than the original and signed by someone else. EDUARDO COSTA 1970." These words can be read as the proposal of the creation of a new work or the description of an existing one; this openness is a key part of *A piece that is…*, whose desire to disturb historical knowledge is explicit. In this work, "Costa suggested stealing history as a political activation of Conceptual practice."[13]

A piece that is… appears in *Art in the Mind,* a 1970 exhibition that existed primarily as a catalogue. Costa originally submitted a proposal for one of his *Fashion Fictions,* but the curator rejected it "perhaps," Costa writes, "because of the then prevalent vision of fashion as a frivolous field, whereas art and conceptualism were serious."[14] *A piece that is…* consists only of text, but by proposing or describing a falsely dated conceptual work and pointing out how easily conceptual art can be imitated, it distances itself from conceptual art as a codified style and from the exhibition catalogue in which it appears. It does more than claim a place for itself in the history of conceptualism, which it aims to undermine. It's already on the move elsewhere, dressed up like a conceptual work on its way to some other party.

Although his *Fashion Fiction* proposal was rejected for *Art in the Mind, A piece that is…* is also a kind of fiction. It describes a work that does not, and may never, exist. In this way, it recalls another source of Costa's art, the writings of Jorge Luis Borges, who was his teacher at the University of Buenos Aires and who remains an important presence in Costa's work. In some of Borges's texts, the description of books takes the place of actual books. As he puts it in the prologue to *The Garden of Forking Paths,* published as the first part of *Ficciones*:

> It is a laborious madness and an impoverishing one, the madness of composing vast books—setting out in five hundred pages an idea that can be perfectly related orally in five minutes. The better way to go about it is to pretend that those books already exist, and offer a summary, a commentary on them… I have chosen to write notes on imaginary books.[15]

For Borges, secondary information—"commentary," just like in Costa and Masotta's *On Happenings*—usurps the place of primary information, the actual text. A fiction can be about some other, non-existent fiction. Conceived in this way, the term "fiction" functions as a subversive synonym for "conceptual" in Costa's works, which are also imbued with the irony that can be sensed in Borges's prologue.

This emphasis on the conceptual, fictional aspects of Borges's and Costa's works does not imply that Borges abandons the task of creating literary texts or that Costa gives up making concrete, physical works of art. There is still a text in Borges: the carefully crafted five-minute story. And Costa's conceptual works are still works: *A piece that is...* has aesthetic qualities, and his *Fashion Fictions* may be about the codes of the fashion media, but they also involve actual objects.

Although he makes clear that he is interested in systems and although he would have learned, even before Masotta started using the term, a lesson in "dematerialization" from structuralism's focus on relations over objects, it would be a mistake to understand Costa's art as dematerialized in any common sense of that term, especially since many of his works could be considered excessively material.[16] There were, for instance, millions of copies published of some of his *Fashion Fictions* when they appeared in magazines like *Vogue*.

Costa has long been interested in rethinking materials and concepts of materiality. His "Volumetric Paintings," begun in the 1990s, are a good example of this. They are about the revolutionary qualities of a relatively new material, acrylic paint, which he uses to make three-dimensional abstract and figurative paintings.[17] His sound works are about suprasegmentals, the qualities of the human voice whose importance is often ignored and in which gender, class, nationality, age, and the body can appear without becoming explicit, without being part of what would usually be called the meaning of an utterance.[18] His *Oral Literature* (1966) and *Tape Poems* (1969) are about the materiality of speech, as is his short silent film *Names of Friends: Poem for the Deaf Mute* (1968), in which he speaks the names of his friends, which remain indecipherable to anyone who can't read lips, and in which the camera, operated by Hannah Weiner, focuses on Costa's mouth as a moving, salivating organ. His "Talking Paintings," made in collaboration with Marta Chilindron, are intended to engage the spectator's concrete experience of the environment of the gallery. All these works focus attention on the material qualities of their mediums.

In a 2015 panel discussion on Argentine art at the Walker Art Center, Costa remarked that, in many conceptual works, "there was no dematerialization, but there was a displacement of materiality," and he suggested that it might be better to think of conceptualism as deferring or thematizing materiality. He went on to say that, although some classic conceptual works didn't have the same kind of materiality as a painting or sculpture, they still took on material form, circulating "in magazines and images that were dissolving into culture."[19] This remark makes clear how Costa's interest in new kinds of materiality is related to another central concern of his work: the questioning of the boundary between art and life. After his mass media art, oral literature, and first *Fashion Fictions*, Costa went on to make more works that were about just such "dissolving into culture," including his contributions to "Street Works," "Usable Art," and *Tape Poems*, and to write about the works of other artists with similar interests, including Marcel Duchamp and Costa's friends Scott Burton, Ana Mendieta, and Hélio Oiticica. For Costa and the poets and artists he knew, aesthetic experimentation went hand in hand with the development of new ways of living, including new forms of romantic and sexual life. Masotta is explicit about this: for him, Pop Art and structuralism are critiques of the "centered subject."[20]

Costa is less polemical than Masotta and his work's concerns too specific to make grandiloquent claims about the subject, but he is interested in using the lessons learned from new forms of art to contribute to the creation of new forms of life, and vice versa. This was already true in his recorded works of oral literature, which for Costa marked a turning point in his activity as a literary author; for him, the act of "recording other people" created "the first poetry that I could say is truly mine" and revealed, in a new way, the aesthetic, literary potential of quotidian language.[21] Costa's proposals for "Street Works" and his contributions to *Tape Poems*, all included here, reflect a desire to intervene directly in the everyday—or, better, to show how everyday life is already, in itself, more than everyday and full of aesthetic and political potential.[22] In his essay "Duchamp: The *Bathtub* or an Assisted Mural Ready-Made," Costa reports on his discovery of a Duchamp work, and he reveals how it stages the interpenetration of the banal (taking a shower) and the mythological (the encounter of Diana and Actaeon).

It's appropriate that Costa's collected writings make up one of the first volumes in a new series of translations published by Les Figues Press. Costa has been a translator in a literal sense, publishing and editing literary translations, and, in the 1969 *Street Works II*, on 14th Street in New York, he inserted handwritten Spanish translations into English advertisements and English-language translations into Spanish advertisements. In "Fashion Show Poetry Event Essay," co-written with John Perreault and Hannah Weiner, "translation" takes on a meaning close to "creation."[23] The implication of translation in his work is even more significant if the sense of translation is taken more broadly to include moving between cultures and between mediums. For decades, his works and his genres have emerged as the result of constant translation among U.S. and Latin American contexts. His exhibition reviews introduced many Latin American artists to Anglophone audiences, and his works, from the very beginning, bear the traces of many cultures, especially Argentine, US, and Afro-Brazilian traditions.[24] This collection aims to make the complexity of Costa's internal translational structures visible, to make them accessible to a new public, so that they might gain a new solidity and permanence, but also so that they can dissolve and disappear in new ways.

NOTES

1. A thorough, bilingual Spanish/English book about Costa was published in 2014 and includes a comprehensive bibliography of his publications and of writings about his work: Laura Buccellato, ed., *Eduardo Costa: Voces, Vida y Obra* (Buenos Aires: Museo de Arte Moderno de Buenos Aires, 2014). A helpful chronological account can also be found in *Eduardo Costa: Volumetric Paintings, The Geometric Works* (New York: Cecilia de Torres Gallery, 2001), 39–59.

2. This is María José Herrera's description of Costa in a 2008 article republished in her *Cien años de arte argentino* (Buenos Aires: Biblos-Fundación OSDE, 2014), 324.

3. On the happening in Buenos Aires, see Andrea Giunta, *Avant-Garde, Internationalism, and Politics: Argentine Art in the Sixties*, trans. Peter Kahn (Durham, NC: Duke University Press, 2007), 185–88; Ana Longoni and Mariano Mestman, *Del Di Tella a "Tucumán Arde"* (Buenos Aires: El Cielo por Asalto, 2002), 68–71; and Ana Longoni and Mariano Mestman, "After Pop, We Dematerialize: Oscar Masotta, Happenings, and Media Art at the Beginnings of Conceptualism," trans. Linda Phillips, in Inés Katzenstein, ed., *Listen Here Now! Argentine Art of the 1960s: Writings of the Avant-Garde* (New York: Museum of Modern Art, 2004), 160–61.

4. "A Mass Media Art," included in this volume. On mass media art, see Alexander Alberro, "A Media Art: Conceptualism in Latin America in the 1960s," in Michael Newman and Jon Bird, eds., *Rewriting Conceptual*

Art (London: Reaktion, 1999), 140–51; Karen Benezra, "Media Art i15n Argentina: Ideology and Critique 'Después del Pop,'" *ARTMargins* 2–3 (2012): 152–175; and María José Herrera, "La experimentación con los medios masivos de comunicación en la Argentina de la década del 60," in *Arte argentino del siglo XX: Premio Telefónica de Argentina a la Investigación en Historia de las Artes Plásticas* (Buenos Aires: Fundación Telefónica, 1997), 71–113.

5. From "On Happenings, Happening: Reflections and an Account," in this volume.

6. Longoni and Mestman, "After Pop, We Dematerialize," 162.

7. Roland Barthes, "Literature Today: Answer to a Questionnaire in *Tel quel*," in Barthes, *Critical Essays*, trans. Richard Howard (Evanston, IL: Northwestern University Press, 1972), 152.

8. On the importance and political stakes of structuralism for Argentine intellectuals in the early 1960s, including Costa's professors at the University of Buenos Aires, Ana María Barrenechea and Salvador Bucca, see Cynthia Acuña, "El itinerario del estructuralismo en la Universidad de Buenos Aires (1958–1966)," *XII Anuario de investigaciones de la Facultad de Psicología, Universidad de Buenos Aires* (2004): 281–87.

9. Roland Barthes, "Blue is in Fashion This Year: A Note on Research into Signifying Units in Fashion Clothing," in Barthes, *The Language of Fashion*, eds. Andy Stafford and Michael Carter, trans. Andy Stafford (New York: Berg, 2006), 46.

10. This was just the beginning of a great deal of international media attention for Costa's *Fashion Fictions* and his jewelry (which, unlike the *Fashion Fictions*, was meant to be worn and was produced by Costa for the designer Carolina Herrera and sold by Henri Bendel and Bergdorf Goodman); see Buccellato, ed., *Eduardo Costa*, 40–49, 67, 72, 75–77, 95–97, 102–113, 118–22.

11. Alexander Alberro, "Reconsidering Conceptual Art, 1966–1977," in Alberro and Blake Stimson, *Conceptual Art: A Critical Anthology* (Cambridge, MA: MIT Press: 1999), xvii.

12. "John Perreault Interviews Eduardo Costa," included in this volume.

13. Miguel A. López, "How Do We Know What Latin American Conceptualism Looks Like?" trans. Josephine Watson, *Afterall* 23 (Spring 2010): 20.

14. Email to author quoted in Patrick Greaney, "Essentially the Same: Eduardo Costa's Minimal Differences and Latin American Conceptualism," *Art History* 37.4 (September 2014): 660.

15. Jorge Luis Borges, *Collected Fictions*, trans. Andrew Hurley (New York: Penguin, 1999), 67, emphasis in the original.

16. On the roughly simultaneous development of the notion of dematerialized art in Argentina and the United States, see Sabeth Buchmann, "Introduction:

From Conceptualism to Feminism," trans. Lucinda Rennison, in Cornelia
Butler, ed., *From Conceptualism to Feminism: Lucy Lippard's Numbers Shows
1969–74* (London: Afterall, 2012), 11–15. In his studies of structuralism in
the late 1950s and early 1960s (and thus long before Masotta's 1967 lecture
"After Pop, We Dematerialize"), Costa would have come across something like
dematerialization. In a 1961 interview published in *Tel quel* and quoted in the
epigraph to Costa's 1965 story "Mental Relations," Barthes writes about the
priority, for him, of "systems" over "objects:" "il s'agit donc plus de systèmes
que d'objets: leur être est dans la forme, non dans le contenu ou la function;"
Roland Barthes, "La littérature, aujourd'hui," in Barthes, *Essais critiques*
(Paris: Gallimard, 1964), 155. And there's a similar emphasis on "relations"
over "*relata*" in many structuralist texts that Costa would have encountered,
including in the preface to a collection of translations edited by Costa's
professor Salvador Bucca for use in the classroom; see Salvador Bucca, *Cuatro
articulos de lingüística estructural* (Buenos Aires: Universidad de Buenos Aires,
Departamento de lingüística y literaturas clásicas, 1962), v. Costa cites Bucca's
recordings of indigenous languages as one of the sources for his interest in
working with spoken language and using a tape recorder. Bucca's work in this
field during the time when Costa studied with him is documented by his 1958
recordings of the Toba and Mocoví languages deposited in the Archives of the
Languages of the World at the University of Indiana, Bloomington.

17. See Alexander Alberro, "Reformulating Modernist Painting: Eduardo
Costa's Geometrical Abstractions," in *Eduardo Costa: Volumetric Paintings, the
Geometric Works*, 9–29.

18. Although most or even all of what is important to Costa in his oral
literature and sound works is lost in the process of transcription, they are
included here so as to provide a print record of these works. The poems
from *Tape Poems* can be heard on UbuWeb (at http://www.ubu.com/sound/
tape_poems.html). My understanding of Costa's sound works has benefited
from two unpublished studies: Tom McEnaney, "Real-to-Reel: The Tape
Poems Anthology of Eduardo Costa and John Perreault," and Nadja Rottner,
"Eduardo Costa's Proposal for an Oral Literature."

19. Eduardo Costa, remarks made as part of the panel discussion "Argentine
Pop and Its Dematerialization," moderated by Bartholomew Ryan as
part of "International Pop Opening Day Talks" at the Walker Art Center,
Minneapolis, April 11, 2015; video documentation can be found at http://
www.walkerart.org/channel/2015/argentine-pop-and-its-dematerialization.
The phrase "dissolving into culture" is a version of the claim that "aesthetics
is dissolving into social life" ("se acabó la contemplación estética porque la
estética se disuelve en la vida social") made on the fourth page of Octavio Paz's
letter to Costa from November 11, 1966, reproduced in facsimile in Buccelato,
ed., *Eduardo Costa*, 31.

20. Oscar Masotta, *Arte Pop y Semántica: Dos conferencias pronunciadas en el Instituto Torcuato Di Tella en septiembre 1965* (Buenos Aires: Centro de Artes Visuales, Instituto Torcuato Di Tella, 1966), 4 and 63. On Pop Art in Argentina and its close relation to mass media art, see María José Herrera, "Argentine Pop Art," in Darsie Alexander and Bartholomew Ryan, eds., *International Pop* (Minneapolis: Walker Art Center, 2015), 85–102.

21. Buccellato, ed., *Eduardo Costa*, 25.

22. On *Street Works*, see Judy Collischan and John Perreault, eds., *In Plain Sight: Street Works and Performances, 1968–1971* (Lakewood, Colorado: The Lab at Belmar, 2008) and Anna Dezeuze, "In Search of the Insignificant: Street Work, 'Borderline' Art and Dematerialization," in Ileana Parvu, ed. *Objets en procès. Après la dématérialisation de l'art 1960–2010* (Geneva: Métispresses, 2012), 35–63.

23. *Airón*, the literary journal he co-founded in 1960, was known for its translations of writers like Robert Creeley (whose poetry Costa translated), Allen Ginsberg, Alfred Jarry, and Henri Michaux. In 1973 and 1974, he edited and translated poetry from the United States for an Argentine university project. On the *Fashion Show Poetry Event*, see Alexander Alberro, "Media, Sculpture, Myth," in José Luis Falconi and Gabriela Rangel, eds., *A Principality of its Own: 40 Years of Visual Arts at the Americas Society* (New York: Americas Society, 2006), 168–77.

24. On the place of Afro-Brazilian traditions in Costa's works, see Alberro, "Reformulating Modernist Painting," 27–29; and Buccellato, ed., *Eduardo Costa*, 86. Costa counts as one of his most influential teachers the Brazilian artist, writer, and priest Mestre Didí, whom he met in 1978 in Rio de Janeiro; see his *Art in America* review "Mestre Didí at Prova do artista" in this volume.

NOTE ON THE TEXTS

If the introductory note to a text lists a Spanish title for the original, then the text has been translated for this volume.

Misspellings and typographical errors have been silently corrected.

References to the illustrations have in most cases been removed from the texts.

Some texts were edited for clarity by Costa and the editor.

Unless otherwise noted, all materials published here for the first time are from Costa's archive.

MENTAL RELATIONS (1965)

First published as "Las relaciones mentales" in Airón *9 (October 1965), 25–27, where it concludes with this note: "This fragment was excerpted randomly from a longer text. It includes a few phrases from Faulkner and from an advertisement in a North American magazine."*

...fashion and literature are perhaps what I would call homeostatic systems, that is, systems whose function is not to communicate an objective, exterior signified which pre-exists the system, but merely to create an equilibrium of operations, a signification in movement: for...the secondary meaning of a literary text is perhaps evanescent, "empty," although this text does not cease to function as the signifier of this empty meaning. Fashion and literature signify strongly, subtly, with all the complexities of an extreme art, but, if you will, they signify "nothing," their being is in signification, not in what is signified.
– Roland Barthes

...and the car veered out of control, crashing against the pillar beneath a bridge and finally stopping, his wife dying not long after, his photo and brief biography appearing in a large book with covers bound in black leather, on which the title *La República Argentina A Principios De Siglo* [The Argentinean Republic at the Beginning of the Century] could be made out in gold letters beneath the national coat of arms, who was carrying an enormous gold watch that later came

to belong to his eldest son, Federico, and then passed from him to his
eldest son, and suits made of wild silk for summer Sundays, his features
with his characteristic nose being found fully ten years after his death
in some laborer harvesting forage perched atop a haystack or in some
nutria hunter or train conductor who might have recalled his youth,
whose father or rather Elena's grandfather and the others in turn took
out the first mortgage on the still intact two square kilometers from a
loan shark from the north, and spent the last forty years of his existence
selling parcel after parcel so as to keep current on the mortgage on the
rest, and finally sold the last that was left of the property except for the
plot where the house was built, the vegetable garden, the stables, and
a few tack rooms converted some time before into a living space for a
girl discovered on a particular day in July beneath a bridge in the frost
and whom they had adopted, teaching her to work as a servant even
after she married and with her whole family, and the land for the rabbit
hutches, the bee boxes and the hens that preceded those red chickens
that later, when everything seemed to flourish again under the hand
and by the effort of the first Bartolo Castro, the people of Navarro,
the settlers, went to see on Sunday afternoons, which were the main
diversion of many people on Sundays, because at that time there was
neither a cinema nor a pastry shop and people
                                        on Saturdays, on
Sundays, didn't know what to do, where to go, the place filled up with
people, men, women, greeting each other, some who hadn't seen each
other for a long time
    "This is María Luisa Castro, I'd like to introduce you to María Luisa
Castro"
    "Nice to meet you, it's a pleasure, nice to meet you"
    "Old buddy, old buddy, how are you, it's been thirty years, thirty
years since I've seen you"
    "And your dad, how's your dad"
    "It's as if it was yesterday, you're the same, you're the same," hugs,
new smiles, excitement
    "Do you remember armadillo barbecue, when your uncle, and my
father, they'd made that bet, about who would win the elections"
    "Ah, yes, the main thing was to have the barbecue, remember, for
them, what they really wanted to do was have the barbecue"
    "This is my sister Ernestina, who never used to go over there, over
to Navarro, she avoided the countryside, and you, did you know her?"

2

"But, it made me so happy, to see them, to see them all together, all of them again"

almost without suspicion, almost without envy or veiled aggression, looking at each other as if they were discovering one another and wanted to contemplate each other for their whole lives, smiling,

"María Elvira is Elena's propagandist, with the telephone, grabs the phone and she'll talk to all of us, she'll tell us how good Elena is, what kind of family she's from, she's talked to all of us over the phone"

"Eduardo, man, wow you look so great, you've taken such great care of yourself, it's as if it was yesterday"

"Elena, answer, it's for you, the phone's for Elena"

"Yes, who is it?"

"Ah, dear, how are you, how is Abby, how is everyone, come over right away, I'm so happy, I want you to come, dear, do whatever you can to come, stop by, put Abby in a cab and come, both of you come over"

forgetting old quarrels, old differences or misunderstandings or old hates and rivalries

on the day of reconciliation, and letting affection, pleasantness, self-love, and love for everyone else flow

"What do you mean she can't, come over, both of you, come, even if it's just for a minute, I can tell Abby's a sweetie, tell her we'll take care of Abby, you should come, we'll have a drink, we'll eat something"

and the bride, exceedingly anxious, agitated, "Something came up last-minute, the hairdresser's, don't tell her, it had to be changed, I don't know, very, too much"

she'd arrived late, after the agreed-upon time, with barely a few minutes to get to the church, where her fiancé and the wedding party and the guests were waiting

—despite being very intimate—a considerable number of people filled the place,

she goes into the house where the party will be held, her older brother's house, where she will get dressed in an elegant wedding dress appropriate for her age, agreeably agitated and hastily, pleasantly impressed

she walks rapidly, and goes into the bathroom without noticing that another brother is in there

"Ay! Get out Bartolito, everyone get out" she sits down on the toilet without looking around her and starts to pee nervously

3

"I have to pee before I put on my dress," without bothering to shut the door,

leaving the door half-open, through which a glimpse of her thighs can be captured, criss-crossed by a garter,

unconcerned with the details, demanding the treatment she deserves given her starring role, taking her place

at the center of the table, the person who should be accompanied, surrounded, encircled, exalted

and, more than anything, should displace everyone else from the places where they've positioned themselves

she leaves the bathroom in her slip, a flesh-colored slip with nylon lace edging, and moves among the servers who are busy bringing glasses and packages of food (pastries, sandwiches, little salads, pickles) to the kitchen

where she asks for a glass of water and then wanders back among the somewhat astonished servers,

she goes into a bedroom where at varying degrees of distance or closeness her sisters and her sister-in-law dress her, surround her, fix her up, get her ready

and almost immediately the guests arrive, they greet one another, they scatter throughout the rooms

"Here, I've brought you a little gift, Elena, a memento, it's a little antique cup, you know I only buy antiques," apologizing for the size of the gift, praising its quality, its virtues that should not be measured with crude measurements "Everything I buy is antique," with a proud and refined smile, proud of her customs and eccentricities, subtly proffering her praise, her propaganda, and that of her entire family and her class

"You can dry all your clothes at the same time, you can wash just once a month, if you feel like it"

"You can't imagine how fantastic they are, the time you'll save"

"I chose it because of that, they're so practical, so practical"

"And your husband has five days to sit in the sun, breathe the salty ocean air, plan his work in peace

and be with you"

"When you travel by sea on the large transatlantic ships you don't lose time,

you save it

(make sure to remember this when you find yourself making the case to your husband about the advantages of traveling by sea),

4

you begin to do things again
together with him
to have pleasant "cocktails" and after-dinner drinks,
discovering once again the light of the moon, dancing until all
hours..
....

First Listening Session of Works Created Using Oral Language (1966)

Co-authored with Roberto Jacoby. First published on a poster for an event titled "Primera audición de obras creadas con lenguaje oral," which took place on October 20, 1966 at the Center for Audiovisual Experimentation in the Instituto Di Tella in Buenos Aires.

All literary works consist principally of a selection of elements from common language, which the writer combines in a unique way. Basically, literary creation always consists of the selection and new combination of familiar elements.

We now propose a new genre that applies the same principles of literary creation to works that stem from oral language. Based on fragments of living language gathered with a sound recorder, we have created, together with Juan Risuleo, "literary" works to be heard directly on tape. As it stores the language that later will be combined to form the work, the recorder functions as something like objective memory, exterior to the artist.

In this way, literature might recuperate all the richness of oral language (tones of voice, the age and sex of the person speaking, perhaps their social class); these are lost when we work with written language.

Oral Literature (1966)

Transcribed and translated from a digital recording of a program that was presented either at the First Listening Session of Works Created Using Oral Language *or as part of the work* Poema ilustrado [Illustrated Poem] *in the exhibition* El poema y su sombra [The Poem and Its Shadow], *curated by Mercedes Álvarez Reynolds at the Galería de Arte Joven de LS1 Radio Municipal, Buenos Aires.*

Excerpt 1:

Woman: When I was seven, no when I was six, it was when I was really really little, in the bed made of bronze (laughs). I laugh because the bed frame had a little knickknack on it that looked like small scissors when it was closed, you know? Made of bronze (inaudible). So it turned out that I took a liking to this man, a dark-skinned guy, and I don't know if that was his last name. What was he like? It's on the tip of my tongue (inaudible). So then, in Papá's large wardrobe, not the wardrobe but rather in Mamá and Papá's bedroom. I was doing my hair in their bedroom, since I was struggling to do it, I knew it wasn't turning out right. I think that afternoon if I had a boyfriend and he were watching me, standing at the door, I know he wouldn't love me because I make such a fuss, I'm so retarded when it comes to doing my hair. But that was totally separate, because there's no reason to talk about that. That's how white I am, too, with no sin whatsoever, with no stain of sin. She says, a feminine voice with a really pretty tone in her voice, she says, "it can't be, it can't be her." I don't know who the voices are, they are feminine and masculine voices. Like a girl with a really nice way about her, really charming. Oof, I'm pretty tired now. All these stories can be told because they say that God loves everyone. And I believed in God the Almighty since I was little, since I was walking around the yard, one time, I don't know if they'd put me on top of an animal, I don't know what animal, its eyes were very large and I put my face closer to the animal's, I lean over a little like this and I was sitting on it, I must've been about a year old at the time, and someone says something to me, I hear something like that, from above, that came from faraway, saying...don't feel bad dear, you'll see how lovely, it says, what will happen to you in your life, something so lovely so lovely.

Excerpt 2:

First Woman: (laughs) I don't know anything, the hen isn't even prancing around because she's getting grabbed here by the neck, like this, and she goes "chik" and that's all. I once tried to kill a hen and I spun it round and round so many times and then I let go and it was still alive, poor thing.

Second Woman: How depressing. Ay ay.

First Woman: And I was shouting: "Don Manuel, Don Manuel" I was shouting at the man. "What's going on, señora? What's going on?" "Ay, look, I was trying to kill a hen and it's still jumping around." And he ran over and grabbed it and killed it. Without saying anything at all, without making a peep or anything. He had experience. When I was a little girl, princes and kings came to see me. When I was a little girl, they came to my house. I remember the Queen of Romania. It's been years since then but I remember it. The Queen of Romania was quite young in those years. She was wearing white. They say she came alone, because I sensed my grandmother saying the Queen of Romania is coming. And they called for me. She's on my mother's side. When I was a little girl they came to my house to see me. It's been years since then but I remember them. I know that the Prince of Wales of England. When I was a little girl, princes and kings came to my house to see me. It's been years since then but I remember them. Yes, years since then. Yes, they came.

Eduardo Costa: An Interview about Oral Literature (1966)

First published as "Eduardo Costa: también la literatura ha muerto" in Confirmado, *October 27, 1966, 74. The new title for this interview—which originally appeared as "Eduardo Costa: Literature Has Also Died"—was suggested by Costa.*

On Thursday, October 20 at six in the evening, the hall of the Centro de Experimentación Audiovisual [Center for Audiovisual Experimentation] at the Instituto Di Tella in Buenos Aires had surpassed its normal capacity. The 240 attendees listened with almost religious devotion to voices, laughter, fragmentary dialogues, a softly intoned song, silences hardly broken by the ticking of an alarm clock transmitted from an imposing Grundig recording device. Once 45 minutes had passed and the listening session was over, Eduardo Costa (26 years old), Roberto Jacoby (22) and Juan Risuleo (20)—all three vaguely connected to the Faculty of Philosophy and Letters of the University of Buenos Aires and co-creators of the experience—were beyond satisfied. They had proposed a new literature, based on oral language as used by contemporary Argentines, and they found no other means to reach their goal than to record conversations and dialogues with strangers, sift through the material, and use these recordings to make what they call an art of oral language. Thus, Pop had arrived to literature. With easel painting abolished, the only thing left was to destroy book literature. A pathway on which fantasy author Ray Bradbury had already set off, in *Fahrenheit 451*.

Eduardo Costa, a 1964 university graduate in Literature and creator of the initiative that has culminated in this new literature, passionately and even stubbornly defended the theoretical suppositions behind this form of art.

CONFIRMADO — *The recordings that you have assembled aspire to be a new literature. What are the reasons behind it?*

EDUARDO COSTA — Written literature cannot transmit what these tape recordings say: the writer omits intonation, silences, even the guttural sounds of the characters. Oral language is much richer than literary language.

C. — *Would the language of Cervantes not be as rich as a recorded dialogue between two characters from the sixteenth century?*

E.C. — That's not what I am referring to: the language spoken now by Argentines is very different from the language writers use.

C. — *Borges said something similar.*

E.C. — But even Borges loses the richness of the spoken language. There is a difference between that elderly woman who tells the story of how she killed a chicken on the tape that we played and what you could say if you were to tell the story of what happened. You would never be able to transmit that atmosphere.

C. — *That's not my problem. Do you write?*

E.C. — Yes, I've published poems in the magazine *Airón* in Buenos Aires; *El Corno Emplumado* in Mexico; *Temas* in Uruguay. At the end of the year, I'll publish a book, *Las relaciones mentales* [Mental Relations].

C. — *At first glance, it seems like a way to avoid the difficulties of actually writing.*

E.C. — No, because they are two different things. When I make recordings, I am interested in the language people use.

C. — *So it's philology, then...*

E.C. — Not at all. A philologist would take note of all of the elements of a language and its combinations. I make a work of art because I select what I record. I publish or transmit what seems beautiful to me, or pretty.

C. — *Beauty... And you already know what that is?*

E.C. — If I knew, I would have half the problems figured out. I record in the street, at parties, in gatherings that seem interesting to me, what ordinary people say in everyday dialogues or monologues, radio broadcasts, anything.

C. — *I understand. And why didn't you record a speech by the President?*

E.C. — Because Onganía does not give speeches, he reads something that's already been written down. Although perhaps I could do it by also recording people's comments about it. That would be a marvelous topic.

C. — *What topics are you interested in?*

E.C. — I'm not interested in topics, or in stories. I just want to make works out of pure oral language. For me, the tape recorder functions like a memory that is exterior to myself: but it is an objective memory, it faithfully preserves the collected material.

C. — *It's practically a return to naturalism.*

E.C. — If you are looking for precursors, I could mention Émile Zola, something like his notebooks.

C. — *Which are not his best work.*

E.C. — That's another matter; besides, Zola has been surpassed. It'd be better to talk about Jean-Luc Godard: he uses a camera to do what we aim to do with the tapes.

C. — *But that's cinema.*

E.C. — Of course: I am not looking for images of people, but rather their language, and I try to transcribe it exactly as it objectively occurs and exactly as it reflects everyday life.

C. — *The French objectists—Robbe-Grillet, Nathalie Sarraute, Michel Butor—make the same claims. But they don't use a tape recorder to make literature.*

E.C. — I admire them. They are my teachers.

C. — *And in Argentina?*

E.C. — Borges, Molina, Girri.

C. — *And Marechal?*

E.C. — No, please. He's phony, an overdone version of all the literary innovations made by other people.

C. — *There are those who would disagree.*

E.C. — Let them get upset. But literary criticism doesn't interest me. I am looking for what is current, this country, the people. What is happening now makes us turn to the past.

C. — *With premises like that you could just as well write some propaganda.*

E.C. — Perhaps, but at any rate a propagandistic writer communicates a new reality using an old language. That's not what I want to do.

C. — *And a recorder allows you to do what you want to do?*

E.C. — Yes.

C. — *At any rate, you won't be making literature.*

E.C. — What does that matter? At least I'm doing something new, something different. When Mujica Láinez listened to the works, he was shocked. He was asking himself where the old writers were going to end up. Though I don't think we're going to kill literature. This is something different and new that has a lot of possibilities. Now other people are also doing recorded works.

C. — *It'll be a fad.*

E.C. — Maybe. In any event, it will be lovely.

Recovery from Chance (1966)

Co-authored with Roberto Jacoby. First published as "Rescate del azar" in Roberto Jacoby, El deseo nace del derrumbe *(Barcelona: Ediciones de la Central, 2011), 53–54. Description of a project titled* Señal de obra *[Sign of a Work] made for the Primer Festival Argentino de Formas Contemporáneas [First Argentine Festival of Contemporary Forms] in Córdoba, Argentina in September, 1966.*

Different parts of the architecture of the city—inside and outside of a gallery: columns, railings, curbs, display windows, benches in plazas—were painted the same color (green). A board of the same color was hung inside the gallery, signaling the existence of the work. During the opening, the display window of a business located across from the gallery was painted the same color.

We began with the existence of two independent codes, one architectural and the other visual-aesthetic; our materials were the creations of the architectural code, insignificant from the point of view of the visual-aesthetic code: they are pure chance.

The introduction of an indicator (color), its repetition, gives aesthetic meaning to the architectural objects. When they are removed from their context, they are recuperated from chance. The color instantiates a new organization of the architectural elements, which begin to form part of another discourse: that of the visual arts.

Each painted part becomes a segment, a unit of meaning, which combines with others to form a new message.

For example, out of the entire range of possible architectural elements, the only ones selected were columns, curbs, benches in plazas, display windows and railings—and nothing else. In addition, these elements were chosen from the entire range of elements of their type that exist in the city. And at the same time, just as in language, they have been combined in order to constitute, as it were, a phrase. This phrase or sequence was superimposed onto those of architecture (that is: the railings on both sides of the stairs appear before or after the entrance, or they appear between two display windows, etcetera), establishing a new order for reading the city. The reading order depends on the place where one is coming from and on one's level of awareness of the new code.

It could be said that just as poetry constructs its messages by executing a transformation in the structure of language, this work transforms the linguistic structure implicit in architecture.

Whatever the reading order or reading direction, this work has a very particular time and space. As a "work of art," it is not inside a gallery, nor is it entirely outside of it. It is made up of discrete objects, but other additional objects could also be included within it (as long as their color were the same green). In any case, it is possible that very soon the color might disappear and the work might cease to exist. There are two moments of reception: one, the moment of noticing the code; another, once the code is apprehended, the moment of moving through the painted elements. Its time and space are discontinuous, so long as the code allows for them to be reconstituted. Perhaps the place and time of this work, then, are purely in the mind and reside in the awareness of the code. This could seem banal: it happens with all language, yet this work seeks to refer specifically to this phenomenon.

Maybe this is what makes a certain re-creation of the work possible, as this page is read. The operation of removing from context, discovered perhaps by Duchamp, acquires a different sign here, since while he, and later Warhol and others, create work through their textual insertion into the institutionalized gallery venue, this—like almost all exhibitions— attempts not to extract the object from its social context, but rather to situate the operations of its creation as an aesthetic message at its place of origin.

This is what we were alluding to when we chose certain architectural forms that referenced primary structures. We were ironically commenting on the fact that these had been extracted or originated through a thought process related to architecture, and that we "reinstalled" them in their place of origin.

A MASS MEDIA ART (MANIFESTO) (1966)

Co-authored with Raúl Escari and Roberto Jacoby. First published as "Un arte de los medios de comunicación (manifiesto)" in Oscar Masotta, ed., Happenings (Buenos Aires: Editorial Jorge Álvarez, 1967), 119–22.

In a mass civilization, the public is not in direct contact with cultural occurrences, but rather is informed of them through the news media. A mass audience doesn't, for example, see an exhibition, doesn't experience a happening or a soccer match, but rather sees a projection of it on the news. Real artistic occurrences cease to have importance in terms of their distribution, since they only reach a scant audience. "To distribute two thousand copies of a work in a big modern city is like shooting a bullet into the air and waiting for the pigeons to fall," said Nam June Paik. In the final instance, consumers of information aren't interested in whether an exhibition took place or not; all that matters is the image that the news media construct out of this artistic occurrence.

In order to constitute itself, contemporary art (pop art, fundamentally) sometimes took elements and techniques from mass media, disconnecting them from their natural context (for example, Lichtenstein with comics, or D'Arcangelo with road signs). In contrast to pop art, we seek to constitute our work inside the media itself. In this way, we propose to deliver to the press the written and photographic report of a happening that has not occurred. This false report will include the names of the participants, information about the place and time the happening took place, and a description of the show that's purported to have occurred, with photos taken of the supposed participants under other circumstances. Thus, the meaning of the work will appear in the way the information is transmitted, the way the non-existent event is "realized" and the differences that might arise among the various versions each news reporter creates of the same event. A work that begins to exist in the very moment the consciousness of the spectator constitutes it as already concluded.

There is, then, a triple creation:

—the composition of the false report;

—the transmission of this report through the media's channels of information;

—the reception on the part of the spectator who constructs— via the information received and according to the significance that information acquires within him—the density of a non-existent reality that he imagines to be true.

We thus push a characteristic of the news media to its ultimate extreme: the derealization of objects. In this way, the moment of transmission of the work is privileged over the moment of its constitution. *Creation consists in allowing transmission to do the work of constitution.*

Currently, the work of art is a combination of the results of a process that begins with the realization of a (traditional) work and continues until that work is converted into material transmitted by the "mass media." We now propose a "work of art" in which the moment of its realization disappears, and in this way we will comment on the fact that these works are, in reality, a pretext for setting the media in motion.

From the point of view of the spectator, there are two possible readings of this type of work: on the one hand, there is the reading of those spectators who trust the media and believe in what they see; on the other hand, there is the reading of informed spectators who are aware of the non-existence of the work being announced.

Thus the possibility of a new genre is opened up: "mass media" art in which what matters is not fundamentally "what is said" but rather *the thematization of the media as media.*

Additionally, this report prepares the second group of readers, "warns" others, and constitutes the first part of the work we are announcing.

Buenos Aires, July 1966.

MASS MEDIA ART:
CREATION OF THE FIRST WORK (1966)

Co-authored with Roberto Jacoby. First published as "Un arte de los medios de comunicación: Realización de la primera obra" in Oscar Masotta, ed., Happenings (Buenos Aires: Editorial Jorge Álvarez, 1967), 115–118.

In May 1966, Roberto Jacoby had planned to create an exhibition that would consist solely of the account of an exhibition; that is, to present, in a gallery, solely the catalogue of an exhibition. The catalogue would contain descriptions of the works, and would also include, as completely as possible, all the characteristic elements of a catalogue: opinions from critics, sketches of the works, etc. These elements, all fake, would be the culmination of the falsity of the very exhibition that had been the origin for the catalogue, and they would simultaneously confirm its apparent reality.

Before undertaking this project, Jacoby thought about the creation of a work (a happening) that might replace the reality of the work with the account of that reality, with the further idea that this report might be presented to the mass media. In this way, what would be achieved (Lawrence Alloway) would be a "change in the place of the moment of creation, situating it within the media."

With the goal of recording this idea, Roberto Jacoby and Eduardo Costa wrote a manifesto in which they posited "A Mass Media Art" and made a first attempt at an analysis of the work they'd proposed to create. This manifesto was published with the additional signature of Raúl Escari, who collaborated on the final version of the piece in July of that year. Their need to record the idea through publication of a manifesto did not benefit the process of creating the work, as some journalists found out that the account that would be presented to them would be false, and avoided publishing pieces related to it.

The first steps toward the creation of the work—which we announced in our manifesto "A Mass Media Art"—consisted of coming up with a list of personalities, who are, in a way, myths disseminated by the mass news media. People who, additionally, might be excited by the idea and who would be easily accessible to us. Of all the people we interviewed only two refused to participate. We planned out the work of trying to convince people with an attempt, first, to get commitments from the most important names, artists who might be excited about the idea and support us. In this way their names would serve as an endorsement for the project, to convince other people, who were less aware of the possibilities and strategies of current art, of the "seriousness" of an endeavor that was built on a lie.

Though we attempted to suggest to all the participants that we were creating a "work of art," we had to backtrack after our first attempts at explaining ourselves. Given the total resistance—nuanced with varying levels of courtesy—that people (who were for us, at that stage, the "material" of our work) offered us, we fabricated explanations that might be more comprehensible. For example, an explanation that we were making an attempt at a sociological experiment, which implied a moral critique of the way that the "mass media" functions, or that we wanted their help to play a prank on journalism, which, with its capacity to modify information, had caused some amount of suffering for many of these people, who were thus pleased to encounter an opportunity for revenge. Principally, the "creative work" we were undertaking at that stage consisted of convincing people about our project. Once we'd made our list, we interviewed the people we had planned to talk with, and asked them to invent their own participation in a supposed happening, which they would claim to have attended and in which each invited artist would claim to have "participated." We immediately wrote up an account of the interventions each participant proposed for themselves, in a report we attempted to write in the style—familiar to journalists—of a press release, though in the most dry and brief way possible. This account was then topped off by a theory designed to satisfy the expectations of a group of journalists who were moderately informed about the theories that two young creators of happenings might produce. This theory was based in the idea—which by then was already a myth—that a happening is characterized by the participation of the audience, and insisted on the experimental nature of our work. We also invented a false name, "Happening de la participación total" ["Total Participation Happening"], which related to the theory we were presenting to the press.

Along with the written account, we also presented a set of thirteen photographs taken by Rubén Santantonín, in different sites: the home of the hairdresser Christian, the home of the Walger family, Teatro Avenida [Avenida Theater], Estudio Galanta [Galanta Studio], Galería Bonino [Bonino Gallery], Zapatería Norde [Norde Shoe Store], Centro de Artes y Ciencias [Art and Science Center], Bar Moderno. The report and the photos were presented to a range of journalists, in an attempt to convince them of their veracity and to induce them to treat the materials as they would any journalistic bit of news that they normally might receive. This was not possible in the majority of cases.

On August 21, the first article based on the false report appeared, in the *El Mundo* newspaper (300,000 copies).

On August 25, an article appeared in the magazine *Gente* (90,000 copies).

On August 29, an article appeared in the magazine *Para Ti*.

On September 19, an article appeared in the magazine *Confirmado* (48,000 copies), which spoke generally about happenings, describing the genre based on the information that appeared in our report.

In October it appeared in the literary magazine *El escarabajo de Oro* (5000 copies).

On October 30, the first article to refute our news story appeared, in the *El Mundo* newspaper.

On November 1, another article appeared in *Primera Plana* (50,000 copies).

On November 10, an article appeared in *Confirmado*.

On November 23, a letter from a reader protesting "pop" experience appeared in the magazine *Inédito*.

On December 7, an article appeared in the same magazine, in reference to the artistic activities of the past year, in which the work was mentioned.

It's probable that more references to our work have been published in other magazines.

We had made an attempt to reach a range of different types of publications with our report: a newspaper, a tabloid, a women's magazine, a general interest publication, a literary journal. *Inédito* and

Confirmado picked up on the news on their own, without our having brought any kind of information to their attention.

With respect to how we might "end the work," we decided we'd consider it over when the first articles clarifying the falseness of our report appeared, as well as some reaction that this clarification might have caused among the public who saw the news article. There wasn't a long wait before that reaction occurred; it took the form of a systematic analysis by a sociologist who gathered some of the public's reactions and produced a text about our experience, mimeographed copies of which he handed out personally.

ON HAPPENINGS, HAPPENING: REFLECTIONS AND AN ACCOUNT (1966)

Co-authored with Oscar Masotta. First published as "Sobre Happenings, Happening: Reflexiones y relato" in Oscar Masotta, ed., Happenings (Buenos Aires: Editorial Jorge Álvarez, 1967), 175–82. The original publication was followed by a section that included the scripts for the happenings; these have not been translated here, and references to the scripts have been removed from the text.

When we met, in April 1966, to plan a series of happenings, some of us were already having doubts about the validity, or the novelty, of the genre. We didn't trust that it would be possible to surpass manifestations of the form that had occurred in the United States, its place of origin. And while the genre had become universalized, and at the same time, exhibited fairly imprecise conceptual limits, we weren't sure we'd avoid repeating something that had already been done, and in a somewhat diluted way.

Later, at the beginning of July, when we notified the press about a happening that had not occurred, we were already thinking about another type of artwork: about working on the "inside" of mass media. In any case, and in a country where everyone was talking about happenings without having seen many, it wasn't such a bad idea to enact one. We began, then, by informing ourselves and soon had become familiar with the work and names of Allan Kaprow, Carolee Schneemann, Michael Kirby, Lucas Samaras, La Monte Young, Wolf Vostell, Robert Whitman, Al Hansen, Dick Higgins, Bazon Brock, Charlotte Moorman, Nam June Paik, Tomas Schmit, Joseph Beuys. As our knowledge increased, we developed a growing impression that the possibilities—the ideas—were all used up. The idea *not* to enact an original happening, then, but rather to bring together in one happening various already realized happenings, seemed to us, suddenly, more important. And at the same time, we'd be able to choose the happenings according to some intention. We quickly found one: the intention to enact a happening that would bring together a group of happenings of different styles, creating a grouping that would function as a commentary on the history of the happening. It would not be a complete history, but certain "hallmarks" would be clearly and specifically outlined. We would make an educational tool. In addition, this history of the happening would be a happening that would be composed of happenings. This would make it a true happening, in the sense that this is how the happening distinguishes itself from theater: various happenings or fragments of happenings presented simultaneously and/or successively constitute a happening, while various works or fragments of works of theater do not constitute a work of theater. Just like certain animals, happenings continue to live if they are divided into parts; and this can be done, as well, in such a way that those parts form groups, as they do at other levels of the biological world, and take the shape of colonies.

A colony of happenings and a history of the happening: nonetheless, the title we chose had nothing to do with either of these ideas. In fact, we had found another idea, one that had actually managed to galvanize us. The title we chose was: "Sobre happenings" ["On Happenings"], with the accent on the first word—that is, the idea of a commentary, an account. We would use a happening to narrate other happenings. Our happening would be a mediator, like a language, of absent occurrences in the past that were no longer in existence. The occurrences, the events, in the interior of our happening, would not be just events, they would be *signs*. To put it another way: we were excited, once again, by the idea of an artistic activity focused on "media" rather than on things, on information about the occurrences and not on the occurrences themselves.

So we formed a team: Roberto Jacoby, Eduardo Costa, Miguel Ángel Telechea, Oscar Bony and Leopoldo Mahler. Masotta would collaborate with us as well. And so we chose the happenings that we would represent, and that as we understood it, summarized a historical progression:

1. *Meat Joy* by Carolee Schneemann;
2. A happening by Claes Oldenburg (we don't know what it was called);

3. *Autobodys*, also by Oldenburg;

4. A happening by Kirby (we don't know the name of this one either).

The chronological order in which these pieces were represented didn't coincide, for practical reasons (places, schedules) with the list above. The order was, instead: 3, 2, 4, 1.

The second happening, the earlier Oldenburg happening, was elegant and speculative, a bit uncomfortable for the audience, and took place in a performance hall, which was simultaneously its subject matter. *Autobodys* was cruder, showy, and noisy, with mechanical elements—insistent wheeled vehicles—and took place in a parking structure. Carolee Schneemann's work spoke of "meat"—human bodies intermingled with fish, chickens, strings of chorizo—and fit well within the dominant trend in France, toward sensual works. It was brilliant and pleasing, and transmitted a certain ancient beauty, which would appeal to lovers of the image. Kirby's work, we felt, was the one that was closest to where we were situated: there were no visual art images in it—or, at least, they faded into the background—but rather mechanical media for the transmission of information: film, photographs. It was a happening in and of information media, though the information was not, in the happening itself, mass information.

In order to reconstruct the happenings, we made use of the following information. The original script for Oldenburg's *Autobodys* was in Michael Kirby's book *Happenings* (London, Sedwick and Jackson, 1965). The original script for *Meat Joy* is located in the magazine *Some/thing* (New York, Winter 1965); the "Notes to Meat Joy," a collection of images and occurrences annotated by the author, are there as well; together with her "French Lessons" (Carolee Schneemann was at that time living in France), these constituted the basis for the tape recording that accompanies the unfolding of the actions. We transcribe here what the author called the "Sequence Diagram" of the happening—that is, the script. As regards the other Oldenburg happening, we had access to the account that appeared in *Art News* (February, 1965), which we transcribed in its entirety. Finally, with respect to Kirby's work, we had Masotta's oral account.

Sobre happenings had been planned as part of a series of two talks and three happenings organized by Masotta, all taking place at the Instituto Di Tella: it would be the last show in the series. Internal difficulties with the schedule established for the performance hall at the

Institute caused us to have to postpone and change the date three times. We intuited that these delays would likely further pique the curiosity of an audience that was not accustomed to seeing happenings, an audience that was affected, at that moment in Buenos Aires, by the publicity that the media had given to the word. We had ordered posters for the event: these were a response to the deaf and intentional misunderstanding of the erroneous publicity produced by the media, changing the title of the happening. On those posters you could read: "Happenings, happenings, happenings." The result: at 9pm on December 6, more than five hundred people gathered in the hall and at the doors of the Institute.

Of the five hundred people, no more than two hundred could enter. *Meat Joy* was performed in an enclosed space, an interior storage space in the Institute's building; the floor of that space, by all estimates, would not hold more than that number. At that initial moment, however, there were no issues with the audience. Two hundred people entered, and in the performance hall we gave instructions for them to go to the parking structure located less than a block from the Institute, on Paraguay Street between Florida and Maipú. The audience in the hall followed the instructions and headed to the parking structure, but they were followed by the audience members who had not been able to enter. Five hundred people thus invaded the parking structure on Paraguay Street; *Autobodys* was transformed into something else entirely. The audience occupied the whole length and breadth of the structure, and the cars were forced to enter slowly, opening a path among the people. The lights and cameras for the TV shows "Sucesos Argentinos" ["Argentine Events"] and "Telenoche" ["TVnight"] made a commotion over each of the actions that was performed. Wherever a spotlight shone, all attention would concentrate. The actions—which attempted to follow the script more or less faithfully—were only seen by the people who were nearby. *Autobodys*, which required an open and uncluttered space, so the wheeled vehicles could glide across the floor, was performed in a space that was completely packed, on a floor on which more than a thousand human feet were arrayed. Once the actions had concluded and the spotlights were dimmed, the people returned to the Institute.

Immediately there were issues at the entrance. Everyone wanted to go in, and the people who had tickets to get in had to laboriously make their way through the tumult of the crowds that were thronging against the door to the performance hall. Upstairs, everything was prepared for the beginning of Oldenburg's second happening. We had respected all the instructions we had read in relation to this work (the only thing missing was a doctor with a mirror, and his actions). The audience, arriving slowly in groups, due to the situation taking place at the door, seemed nervous, annoyed. When everyone had managed to enter, pretty much immediately the prohibition against sitting down was disobeyed: the audience occupied the seats.

Meanwhile, from the booth in the hall, using a microphone, we explained the idea of the happening. We offered information about the artists and the actions involved in each of the original happenings and we said—and this was true—that our intention was not to repeat happenings, but rather to produce, for the audience, a situation that resembled that experienced by archeologists and psychoanalysts. Starting from a set of *remains* preserved in the present, they must reconstruct a past, an original situation.

Once the prohibition against sitting down was broken, the happening ended. With people already occupying the theater seats, we quickly began our repetition of Kirby's work. Of this piece, we had retained only what was essential. We had made a film of the people on the creative team in the Bar Moderno, their walk from the bar to the Institute, and of this same group inside the Institute. We combined the film with slides of the same people—ourselves—and with the repetition live onstage of the scene at the table in the bar. We superimposed a recording over the films and slides, reproducing a conversation that accompanied the visual exhibition. As the audience members immediately understood that the artists responsible for the happening were the same people they were seeing on-screen, and as the prevailing feeling was a sensation of discomfort and annoyance, they initially attempted to make their negative assessment known. But the recorded dialogue quickly dampened their mocking intentions: the recording at the very least accounted for audience conduct, acknowledging that they would be attending the happening. And it was said, as well, that they didn't have much belief in happenings, that the genre was dead or past its prime, yet that they recognized that somehow the audience would attend anyway. From that point forward, people were hooked, and followed the rest of the projections attentively. The last was the filmed rehearsal for *Meat Joy*. People were told that what they were seeing projected in sixteen millimeters was a rehearsal for the happening they'd see immediately following the film. In the rehearsal, the performers had not worked with fish or with chickens, but rather with whatever objects were at hand—balls, pieces of wood. In a daring shot, one of the female performers, slowly and suggestively, bit and licked a piece of wood. Then the audience was invited to climb the stairs up to the storage space where *Meat Joy* would be performed.

From the first moment, the audience followed the actions with fascination: the undressing, the intertwining of bodies, the painting, the cut paper, the actual presence of chickens and fish, the smell. The photographers were perhaps a bit crazed. They intermingled with the performers and undeniably became part of the show. It would not be wrong to think that they thought they were in the presence of something truly spectacular. Though perhaps they realized, in some way, that it wasn't so very spectacular. In any case, they did everything possible to make it so. We're referring to the cameras from "Sucesos Argentinos"—within a week, you could see on the news a series of fairly good images of *Meat Joy*, accompanied by the mellifluous and policing voice of a female news commentator, who called on the "authorities" to intervene lest any representations of this type should continue.

Steps Towards Tomorrow: Eduardo Costa Interviewed by Ángel Núñez (1967)

Transcribed from a digital copy of the El paso a mañana: Un ciclo del Instituto Torcuato Di Tella *radio program from December 15, 1967.*

AN: Our last interview of this week devoted to contemporary poetry and literature is with Eduardo Costa, a writer and graduate in literature and letters. He has recently returned from a trip through the United States and a number of places in Latin America, and he's studied some provocative aspects of the current context of literature in the Americas. First of all, we'd like to ask you, Costa, for a general perspective you might be able to share about the literary landscape in the places you have visited, and also about Argentine literature from an outside perspective, which you've perhaps attained.

EC: Well, I think that the problematics might perhaps be divided between South Americans and North Americans, though increasingly it's clear that the problems are universal with respect to literature. With respect to the countries that are usually called underdeveloped, I can still see a kind of persistence, in a certain way, of books and traditional forms of literary transmission, and that these places are being left behind because they're a bit delayed, that is, they're taking their time to abandon these forms. I think this is specifically a little bit of the problem in South America; now, the problem in North America is having recognized, somewhat, the expiration of those forms of transmission of literary material, but not having yet found something to replace them.

AN: Not even in a provisional way? You're talking about replacements. In what way might we experience the replacement of the book, which is, in our community today, the exclusive form of transmission for literary material? What, then, is this form in the United States?

EC: There is a lot of reliance on illustrated weeklies, for instance, and even on radio transmissions with pieces or works written especially for radio transmission, and many writers devote their energies to writing, for instance, scripts for films, and that is another way of making it possible for literary material to reach people on a bit more of a mass scale. I think that this problem is old. And it's been denounced or announced by El Lissitzky, a Russian writer from around 1920, more or less, and he basically announced the displacement of the book by illustrated weekly magazines. At this moment we can see this phenomenon fairly clearly in the United States and it's beginning to be seen in South America as well. In the United States, the best literary works, in addition to coming out in books with limited print runs, are published in illustrated weeklies and even in fashion magazines, for example in *Harper's Bazaar* or *Vogue*, which have fiction sections where the best literary works in the world appear, in the best U.S. translations.

AN: What you're saying to us, wouldn't that lead us to think that the book isn't being replaced, but rather that parallel media are also being utilized?

EC: Well, I think so. That is precisely my opinion. What is by now, we might say, old, is the idea that each new communication medium that appears includes and replaces the other. Which is to say, rather, the theory that is accepted now and that I share is that all these media coexist. What happens is that some become more important, numerically speaking, more massive and hence more powerful—even economically—than the others. That is, clearly the power to reach an audience and the power of a business that's behind an illustrated weekly is more important than the structures behind a book, behind each volume that appears. Now, in general, the publishing houses, which are what is behind each volume and each illustrated weekly, they publish, and we might say, they reflect in their very structure the ambiguity that exists in this moment in these two media, and they publish both things.

AN: You made a few references to a point that I'd be interested to delve into with you in a bit more detail. What are the consequences you were able to observe and that you can foresee as a result of this transplanting of media or rather this parallelism of media in the literary situation?

EC: Well, literature, logically, will have to change along with the medium itself—or we might say, with the foundation on which it is conceived and for which it is conceived, which in general in our context is the book, which itself changes as well, that is to say, when that foundation changes. When we no longer write for a book but rather for an illustrated weekly, then we probably will introduce different elements into the work—for instance, photographs, which are characteristic of illustrated weeklies. So we will no longer conceive of literary works solely in terms of written texts, but rather, for example, we'll conceive of them with photos or with other elements.

AN: Don't you think that this might result in a deterioration in the quality of literary endeavors?

EC: No, not at all. Quality has nothing to do with the materials or medium we work with. That would be like thinking that just because a sculptor works with plastic instead of working with marble, his work will be worse. It will be neither worse nor better. That depends on other things, not on the chosen material.

AN: But can we speak here, and using the example of the sculptor, about perhaps proposing a kind of hybrid combination of elements to use?

EC: Yes, of course. If we were to use, for example, in a literary work, written text and photographs, we might be positing a clear hybrid, but that doesn't negatively affect the quality of the work. We know that from other art forms—film itself can be considered a hybrid of literature, image, and other things. And that doesn't necessarily indicate a reduction in its quality. Those are two separate problems.

AN: Eduardo Costa, one last question. Doesn't it seem to you that in the Republic of Argentina we are currently experiencing a boom from the point of view of book distribution, and that this might be an important preparatory stage that we should accept, and that in addition it's one we need to experience before we reach that stage of new forms of distribution to which you've been referring?

EC: Yes, I think so. I think, further, that if we analyze the phenomenon of the American novel and of some large print runs that have taken place, even with Argentine books, we'll see that these large print runs have been achieved thanks to the support given by other forms of media, like for example the magazines that have publicized them, commented on them, and recommended them. Now we're still in a stage when magazines put themselves at the service of the book, to support the book, and they haven't delineated a magazine-based literature that in and of itself might serve as literature. In other words, the literature that we see here in magazines in general is inferior to the literature we might find in some books. But I think this could eventually be transformed.

AN: Thank you very much, Eduardo Costa, for these assessments, you're very kind.

SIX ABSENCES (1968)

Typescript. This is the introduction included in the typescript: "Performed on different dates by Vito Acconci, Scott Burton, Bernadette Mayer, John Perreault, Anne Waldman, and Hannah Weiner, as part of "Theater Works," Hunter College, May 1969. The work was a set of 20 large file cards with one paragraph typed in capitals on each card. It was meant to be performed (read) by anybody except the artist." Costa conceived of the work in 1968.

CARD #1
MY NAME IS EDUARDO COSTA. I WAS BORN IN BUENOS AIRES, ARGENTINA, IN 1940.

CARD #2
AT THE AGE OF FIVE I STARTED ELEMENTARY SCHOOL. I ATTENDED A CO-ED NUN'S SCHOOL FOR TWO YEARS. THEN, I WENT TO A BOYS' PUBLIC SCHOOL.

CARD #3
I STUDIED ENGLISH AT THE ARGENTINE-U.S. CULTURAL INSTITUTE IN BUENOS AIRES.

CARD #4
FROM 1952 TO 1957 I WENT THROUGH HIGH SCHOOL.
FOR ABOUT A YEAR I TOOK VIOLIN CLASSES WITH A
GERMAN REFUGEE WHO HAD BECOME A FRIEND OF
MY MOTHER'S. AT ONE POINT MY TEACHER GAVE UP
TEACHING TO GET MARRIED.

CARD #5
FOR TWO YEARS I TOOK DRAWING AND PAINTING
CLASSES WITH A TALENTED PRIVATE TEACHER FROM
ITALY WHO HAD RECENTLY MOVED TO BUENOS AIRES.

CARD #6
IN 1958 I STARTED COLLEGE. I ATTENDED THE
UNIVERSITY OF BUENOS AIRES, WHERE I TOOK
LITERATURE, AND ALSO ART, PSYCHOLOGY, AND
SOCIOLOGY.

CARD #7
ONE OF MY TEACHERS WAS JORGE LUIS BORGES, WITH
WHOM I TOOK ENGLISH AND U.S. LITERATURES. HIS
COURSE WENT FROM THE ANGLO-SAXON SAGAS TO
POETS LIKE BLAKE AND TENNYSON, AND THOMAS GRAY,
AND THEN POE AND WHITMAN.

CARD #8
IN COLLEGE I WAS ONE OF THE EDITORS OF A LITERARY
MAGAZINE. WE PUBLISHED AVANT-GARDE WORK
BY LOCAL WRITERS INCLUDING OURSELVES, AND
INTERNATIONAL WRITERS FROM NATHALIE SARRAUTE TO
ALLEN GINSBERG.

CARD #9
I STARTED A FRIENDSHIP WITH OSCAR MASOTTA, A
BRILLIANT DROP-OUT FROM THE SAME UNIVERSITY WHO
MADE A LIVING BY TEACHING ADVANCED COURSES ON
ART, PSYCHOANALYSIS, AND PHILOSOPHY.

CARD #10
IT WAS GREAT TO HAVE BORGES AND MASOTTA AS
TEACHERS. BORGES IS GREAT WITH THE CLASSICS AND
IS HIMSELF ONE OF THEM. MASOTTA LIKES ROLAND
BARTHES AND MCLUHAN, AND CAN REALLY TEACH THEIR
WORK. HE ALSO LIKES TO DISCUSS WARHOL, AND OTHER
ADVANCED ARTISTS.

CARD #11
IN 1965 I GRADUATED WITH AN MA IN LITERATURE.
I ALSO STARTED TO MAKE SOME ART, AND TO MAKE
FRIENDS WITH MANY ARTISTS WHO USED TO MEET AT
THE CAFES NEAR THE UNIVERSITY.

CARD #12
WITH MY FRIENDS RAUL ESCARI AND ROBERTO JACOBY,
WE MADE THE FIRST WORK OF WHAT WE CALLED "MASS
MEDIA ART." WE GAVE THE PRESS A SET OF PHOTOGRAPHS
OF LOCAL CELEBRITIES AND WE TOLD THEM THE
SHOTS WERE TAKEN AT A SOCIALITE'S PLACE WHERE A
HAPPENING HAD BEEN PERFORMED. THE STORY WAS
FALSE, AND THE PHOTOGRAPHS HAD REALLY BEEN SHOT
AT DIFFERENT LOCATIONS. THE PRESS COVERED OUR
"NON-HAPPENING" AS IF IT HAD REALLY TAKEN PLACE,
USING OUR PHOTOS AND VERSION OF EVENTS.

CARD #13
THREE MONTHS LATER WE PUBLISHED IN THE MAIN
MEDIUM THAT HAD TAKEN OUR STORY AN EXPLANATION
OF OUR WORK BY A WELL KNOWN SOCIOLOGIST.

CARD #14
IN 1965 MY FATHER PASSED AWAY AND IN 1966 I RECEIVED
A MODEST INHERITANCE. PART OF IT WAS A CAR. I DROVE
IT SEVERAL TIMES AND HAD SEVERAL MINOR CRASHES.

CARD #15
I SOLD THE CAR AND USED THE MONEY TO COME TO
NYC, WHERE I STAYED FOR THREE MONTHS. I MET MANY
INTERESTING PEOPLE IN NY, AMONG THEM MEXICAN
WRITER OCTAVIO PAZ, AND FASHION DESIGNER CHARLES
JAMES.

CARD #16
ON MY RETURN TO BUENOS AIRES I STARTED TO WORK
ON *FASHION FICTION I* WITH SIGNIFICANT HELP FROM
JUAN RISULEO. THIS WAS A SET OF PHOTOGRAPHS WITH
THEIR COPY WHICH PRESENTED AS REAL A FICTIONAL
COLLECTION OF JEWELRY. THE SET WAS GIVEN TO THE
FASHION MEDIA IN BUENOS AIRES, AND A FEW PHOTOS
WERE PUBLISHED AS IF THEY WERE REAL JEWELRY.

CARD #17
IN COLLABORATION WITH ROBERTO JACOBY AND JUAN
RISULEO I ALSO PRESENTED THE FIRST WORK OF WHAT
WE CALLED "AN ART OF THE ORAL LANGUAGE." THIS
WORK CONSISTED OF TAPES OF CONVERSATIONS WHICH

WE EDITED AND PRESENTED TO A SEATED AUDIENCE
AT THE AUDITORIUM OF THE DI TELLA INSTITUTE IN
BUENOS AIRES.

CARD #18
IN 1967 I CAME BACK TO NYC FOR A MONTH AND
SHOWED *FASHION FICTION I* TO LEO CASTELLI WHO
LIKED IT VERY MUCH BUT DIDN'T SEE HOW HE COULD
USE IT AT HIS GALLERY. HE SENT ME TO ALEXANDER
LIBERMAN OF *VOGUE* WHO IMMEDIATELY HAD IT
PHOTOGRAPHED FOR HIS MAGAZINE.

CARD #19
IN 1968 MY FICTIONAL JEWELRY WAS PUBLISHED IN
VOGUE, AND PRESENTED AS REAL JEWELRY. I CAME AGAIN
TO NY. I MET THE ARTISTS AND POETS IN THIS PROGRAM
AND WE BECAME FRIENDS.

CARD #20
WE COLLABORATED IN SEVERAL PROJECTS. RECENTLY
I WAS INVITED TO PARTICIPATE IN THEATER WORKS AT
HUNTER. THANK YOU FOR COMING. THANK YOU VERY
MUCH.

For an Oral Language Art (1969?)

Typescript from a lecture given in the United States (possibly at Yale University, where Costa also read his story "Mental Relations" or at Columbia University) in the late 1960s.

Every writer, when creating a literary work, unconsciously performs the operation of choosing elements from the whole of language kept in his memory and combining them in a new way.

So we can say that every creative literary task is first of all a selection made from a common material that has been kept by the writer inside his memory. I now propose a new genre, related to literature because it derives from the same material, language, but which we should not call "literary" because its materiality is not written but oral language.

The materiality of literature is the printed letter—written language—and, usually, paper; the materiality of our art works is recorded oral language and tape. For this I do not intend to say that my works are more realistic or directly related to the original oral language—which is not necessarily a virtue—but that in my works language is restricted by a different code, the one formed by all the possibilities created by tape recorders and recording laboratories.

The "literary" works to be heard directly from tapes can be created—or organized—using recorded fragments of living languages. This genre admits the possibility of working with every kind of oral language: conversations, speeches, TV or radio broadcasts, etc.

Oral artists could work in the following way: first they could select what they are going to tape—for instance, as we did for one of the tapes in the *First Listening Session of Works Created Using Oral Language* (Buenos Aires, 1966), a monologue of a mad woman; then, once this basic material is taped, they could make a second selection from that material, keeping only the parts they want to combine in the third step, the most specific of this tape-recorder art: the montage of the tapes, which allows the artist to activate the meaning, syntax, even morphology of the first recorded fragments of oral language. There could be yet another step, involving the use of recording laboratories: it is possible for the artist, thanks to certain technical achievements, to introduce a lot of variations in the different parameters of the voice (speed of the sound waves, pitch, volume). This fact enables us to make, for instance, an artwork that is a tape with any recorded monologue of any person, whose voice changes during the tape from that of a child to that of an old man, from a woman to a man, etc. In such a work a certain reality (the ageing of a person or a sexual change) would be "told" through a change in the quality of the voice (in the speed of the sound waves)—which you can easily do in a laboratory.

Besides, while working with recorded oral language, it becomes possible to recuperate for literature the whole richness and complexity of information that is contained in the original oral language (states of soul of the speaker, emotions, sex, age, social class, geographical origin) and that is easy to discern in the intonation, tones of voice, pronunciation—which we call in linguistics the "suprasegmental features of language"—all of which written language does not allow us to transmit.

We should then make—in order to achieve an oral language art work—a conscious selection from the first corpus of recorded material, and an equally conscious combination (with the whole material in front of us) of the selected fragments, using the technique of montage. The tape recorder functions in this kind of work like a memory outside the artist that has the peculiarity of being quite objective, remaining true to the recorded material, without the alteration that it unavoidably undergoes inside a personal memory.

THE FASHION SHOW POETRY EVENT ESSAY (1969)

Co-authored with John Perreault and Hannah Weiner. First published in 0–9, 5 (1969), 53–55. The Octavio Paz epigraph is from Paz's letter to Costa from November 11, 1966, reproduced in Laura Buccellato, ed., Eduardo Costa: Voces, Vida y Obra (Buenos Aires: Museo de Arte Moderno de Buenos Aires, 2014), 31. The Claude Lévi-Strauss epigraph was invented by the authors, based on his statement in Tristes tropiques that "writing...had allied itself with falsehood [perfidie]."

January 14, 1969, 5:30 and 7:30
Center for Inter-American Relations, 680 Park Avenue, New York, N.Y.

Poetry (Fashion Commentaries) by: Eduardo Costa, John Perreault, and Hannah Weiner

Fashion works by: James Lee Byars, Enrique Castro-Cid, Eduardo Costa, Allan D'Arcangelo, Rubens Gerchman, Alex Katz, Les Levine, Nicholas Krushenick, Roberto Plate, Marisol, Sylvia Stone, Andy Warhol, Susana Salgado, John Perreault, Marjorie Strider, Claes Oldenburg, James Rosenquist, Hannah Weiner, Alfredo Rodríguez Arias, and Juan Stoppani

Music by: Davin Seay and Diane Kolisch

"There is no more aesthetic contemplation because aesthetics is dissolving itself into social life." – Octavio Paz
"Clothing introduced perfidy into civilization. But without clothing could they [the primitive peoples] have taught themselves to think?" – Claude Lévi-Strauss

We see the *Fashion Show Poetry Event* not as a time-bounded work of literature, but as the initial cause of a series of events which are a set of translations that add up to a total work.

Some of these additional events are *The Fashion Show Poetry Event #2*—a recreation using video tapes, slide projections, and stereo tapes—and the *Fashion Show Poetry Event Book* which will be a "documentation" in words and photographs including the texts of our fashion description poems, our press releases, magazine articles, etc.

It might have been interesting for us to have asked the artists to tell us orally an idea for a fashion garment and then for us to have written our texts without making and showing the real garments.

However, some of the reasons we chose to make the effort of presenting an actual fashion show were: to move outside the limitations of the printed word, to move away from personal expression, and to present a fictionalized version of a real life event that would appeal to an audience accustomed to sophisticated perception of visual phenomena.

Rather than attempt a union of our three separate styles we have chosen an objective mass-media style. This makes a difference of kind rather than of degree between our present effort and other forms of literary collaboration.

Concerning the total phenomenon of fashion as a language, we would locate the *Fashion Show Poetry Event* in the area of that particular sub-category of fashion language that could be characteristic of the moment of communication between fashion press and fashion show to consumer.

Fashion language is a complicated code. It has special meanings within the industry itself, involving the translation of exact equivalents, and special meanings when the industry relates to the public.

There are various verbal (written and oral) to visual and visual to verbal translations that take place in the *Fashion Show Poetry Event*.

We wish to indicate some differences between translation and communication. In the process of communication there is a sender, a message, and a receiver. Between sender and receiver some modification of the message may take place even though, for instance, the message is in the English language which is known equally to both sender and receiver.

On the other hand, translation is a process of converting a message from one code system to another (from one medium to another or one language to another).

We communicated to the artists our generalized instructions. They translated these instructions into sketches, models, and finally actual garments. The feedback (i.e. the garments) was then translated by us into fashion language. We have also translated this information into the language of press releases aimed at both the general and the fashion press and into the language of this theoretical essay.

This process of translation is one of the most important subjects of *The Fashion Show Poetry Event.*

The message received by the usual fashion audience and by most of the poetry and art audience as well will be mainly a certain set of meanings. The real message and the message we intend, however, is the game or play of the significants that will transmit an additional set of meanings. There is a difference between a description and that which this description appears to describe. We are interested in this difference. There is a difference between real fashion copy and our "poems" which are imitations of fashion copy.

There is a difference between a real fashion show and our imitation of a fashion show. We are interested in these differences in spite of the fact that we have tried to eliminate them.

We want to show the difference between presentation and representation by bringing presentation and representation as close together as possible.

The Fashion Show Poetry Event is not only fashion, poetry, and art, it is where these arbitrary categories overlap and as categories dissolve and become irrelevant.

The Fashion Show Poetry Event is a new kind of theater.

Theater is a fictional representation of something that supposedly happened in the past or something that is happening in the present. A real fashion show is a fictional representation of something that is going to happen in the future. The *FSPE* is a fiction of this kind of fictional representation.

In theater, costumes are usually subservient to plot and characterization. In the theater of the *FSPE*, as in a real fashion show, the costumes are the plot.

We caused fashion garments to be created by the artists so that we would have a pretext to write the style of fashion.

We use the phrase "write the style" rather than the more usual "write in the style" because the latter indicates that one is using a style to serve a certain content, but here we are writing a certain style using a certain content as a pretext to write this style.

Not only are we writing the style of written fashion language, we are also doing the style of a fashion show. This makes our work a poetry event instead of a poetry reading.

Because the *Fashion Show Poetry Event* is amusing does not exclude the fact that it is also serious. Amusement and beauty in this work are nothing but the condition of the style we are writing and doing, as is fashionableness.

The fact that the audience and we ourselves will find this work amusing is also amusing.

Doing a fashion show is fashionable. The artists we have chosen are fashionable. Poetry events are fashionable. Fashion is fashionable. Fashionableness is not our goal. Our goal is complete objectivity.

The Fashion Show Poetry Event Poems (1969)

Co-authored with John Perreault and Hannah Weiner. First published in Judy Collischan and John Perreault, In Plain Sight: Street Works and Performances: 1968–1971 *(Lakewood, Colorado: The Lab at Belmar, 2008). The texts were written collaboratively by the three artists and poets based on designs submitted by artists for the* Fashion Show Poetry Event *and then read during the fashion show. Excerpts were published as "The Poets Will Provide Her Clothes" in* Harper's Bazaar *(April 1969): 154–55, whose editors decided to present the text as if it were written in verse.*

I

Strange shapes invade the city and the countryside. Yellow and green structures move about when least expected. Surprise! They're not from outer space; they're dresses from South America. A house is not only a home. Rubens Gerchman surely thought of this in making his dress houses… Combine the latest in fashion with the latest in architecture. Wear your home.

II

The ten minute dress! Alex Katz, famed for his cut-out portraits, cuts out this quick party dress in glimmering green for blonds. The two-piece ensemble includes a panel skirt that leaves the midriff bare and a square of the same translucent fabric is tied like a scarf behind the neck. Do-it-yourself elegance! But…signed by Alex Katz… Voila! An original work of art!

III

Stop! Look! Listen!… Go! High-speed, superhighway roadscapes by Allan D'Arcangelo travel into high fashion with this super-chic warrior dress. Modeled by Allan's lovely wife Sylvia, this dress bars not only the bare essentials... Yield... Soft shoulders... Proceed with caution... Detour ahead... Perfect for summer cocktails, poolside promenades, chi-chi openings. Wear one to Allan's opening next month at the Fischbach and watch everyone travel at high speed in your direction.

IV

In a sophisticated act of infidelity to her well-known style, Marisol surprises us with this $10,000 painting to wear. Rene Ricard, poet and film-star, models this hand-painted body stocking... Do you want to be "in"? Do you want to be totally "now"? Do you want to stand out in a crowd? Go dancing or even walking in this eye-catching, slightly insolent creation made especially for the young man about town.

V

Plug into your environment with Jim Rosenquist's suit of adhesive tentacles. What usually happens in your mind will now happen to your clothes. Are you too attached to your environment? Is it hard to get up and go? See how difficult it is for Frank to go from one place to another... This suit will make you aware of the way you feel.

VI

And now poet Eduardo Costa offers two variations of his famous jewelry. Let's look first at Haru Wells, who presents Eduardo's classic rings and earrings. Pure gold custom-molded to your fingers and ears! And next Sheyla comes, wearing a custom-molded, gold brassier. Wear the shape of your own beauty! Classic! Elegant! New!

VII

Taking a trip? Wear your luggage, don't carry it! Poet Hannah Weiner designs this trip cape in shiny blue plastic with multi-rows of locked pockets that snap off, snap on! Leave them in your hotel, carry one as a purse, or snap them all on when you take off! Waterproofed for sudden rainstorms, for packing make-up. Little pockets inside pockets confuse customs! Note the color-coordinated Contac lining. Poet Bernadette Mayer also models the matching bikini and bra.

VIII

Wear your hair in a totally different way! Poet John Perreault demonstrates his exciting "Hair" Line, as modeled by poet Anne Waldman. The chic primitivism of these hair inventions, for full fashion impact, must be worn with the bold, bold, totally new bald-look. No make-up, no hair! Flesh is the message. Two units of long brown hair are all you need for a complete wardrobe. Tied around the head, they become a veil or a hat; tied under the arms, they become a summer blouse that's all sleeves; tied around the body, just above the breasts, they become a daring mini-dress.

IX

From our exotic friends south of the equator, Alfredo Rodríguez Arias and Juan Stoppani, we have a dress created by the marriage of words, colorful fabric scraps, and real fruits and flowers. As the model walks by, let the designer in you create the dress you have always dreamed of.

X

Plastic-man strikes again! Les Levine introduces a luscious line of plastic wearables. Throw away your jewels! These new plastic creations are a light-show to rival your diamonds. They project the real you: sheer, scintillating energy and light. First we have oodles of clear plastic tubes, designed, of course, to reveal more than they expose. These slinky tendrils dangle, dazzle, and broadcast rays of intriguing come-touch-me energy.

For everyday wear, here or on any planet, choose this simple swinging space-age tunic to be worn over earthlier togs or just plain skin. This three-piece marvel of design engineering includes belt and face disc. The super-shiny surfaces reflect ever-changing splashes of light.

Another interplanetary suggestion: aluminum-coated Mylar hoods provide head coverage for introverted nudists and extroverted heads. Have privacy in public; walk in your own mirrored world.

Last but definitely Les Levine at his best in this optical fiber fantasy, perfect for photographs and for that moment when every molecule of you is transformed into pure energy and light. Zap! Sparks of light streak up and down this explosion of plastic antennae.

XI

Have you ever thought of yourself as a work of art? Well, you are. Marjorie Strider's airy mini-length dress frames your frame from every angle to show off every curve. Indulge yourself! At home is the place for the no-holds barred approach to fashion individuality. This dress says a lot about you and a lot about art. Are the parts equal to the whole? Does framing attract or detract? Are you a voyeur? Would you rather look than touch?

XII

And now let's say hello again to Sylvia D'Arcangelo, wearing husband Allan's gorgeous highway landscape dress. The arrow and the highway, typical of his earlier paintings, point to a future mode. Incorporate the excitement of art with the body-consciousness of high fashion!

XIII

Claes Oldenburg makes thoughts about clothes more real than clothes... We quote from Claes Oldenburg's instructions: "A tall naked model with extravagant coiffure and wearing only white high-heel shoes and a soft white blindfold makes her way cautiously down the runway... The poets will provide her clothes..."

This white slave outfit is modeled by Carolee Schneemann who wears a white blindfold, white earrings, and a matched white pearl necklace in the neckline of her see-through white silk blouse. White crepe culottes fall from white satin cumberbund. The white-on-white embroidered white leather vest is made of the same soft material as the white high-heel shoes.

XIV

Now you no longer need to gain weight to feel protected. Enrique Castro-Cid's stuffed green dress allows you to imitate any weight you want. The artist confesses it was a little girl stuffing pillows inside her dress in order to imitate Oliver Hardy that inspired him... In addition, this "body mask" is just right for those difficult transitional moments when your clothes are being altered to match the alterations in your figure.

XV

Let modesty prevail! Look nude but be completely covered! Zip into this second skin of flesh-colored plastic... Roberto Plate introduces his doll-look, complete with matching make-up for knees and elbows. Have one made to order to fit your measurements... Also available in individually matched shades of black, yellow, and red.

XVI

Candy. I call my sugar Candy, because my sugar's sweet on me... Sculptress Sylvia Stone creates the perfect dinner dress! Elegant enough for black-tie affairs, the bodice of this delicious black and white creation is constructed of hundreds of individually sewn Pep-O-Mint Life Savers. The skirt is edible too: long strands of black licorice complement the licorice hair-piece.

XVII

Going to a party tonight? Which sex will you be? Andy Warhol now lets you choose your sex as you choose your clothes. Gerard Malanga, poet and underground filmmaker, models Andy's silvery female torso, perfect when worn with leather for that look of tough-chic... The ultimate Pop solution to the question: is life a drag?

XVIII

For that big moment in your life when you walk down the aisle, wear this hair bow and nothing else... Thousands of bows could have been made from the billowing white tulle that fashions this Alice in Wonderland bow, with a long, long gossamer train. Susana Salgado takes what is normally an accessory and makes it the whole costume. Gigantically ultra-feminine, this vision of purity floats by...

XIX

And now for our grand finale, you the audience are going to model The World's Biggest Hat by James Lee Byars, well-known creator of spectacular group clothing. Group therapy... Group living... And now group clothing... Here's a specially condensed edition of "100 In A Hat" carefully constructed of yards and yards of vat-dyed, acid red, taffeta acetate...

Letter from New York (1969)

First published as "Carta de Nueva York," Sur 316 (January–April, 1969), 146–50. Words in italics appear in English in the original.

Finally, writers seem determined—at least in New York—to enter into a terrain consistently denied to literature: the creation of an avant-garde. It is a relief to see just how much the younger people have changed in regards to the positions they held just four years ago. At that time, they worked to publish a few journals, perhaps some books, and periodically they would hold readings of their work that consisted of simply reading their poetry or prose before an audience. While dancers had distanced themselves from ballet, painters from paintings and theater people from shows and the stage, writers remained devoted to their relationship with the main literary mediums. Nevertheless, the situation began to change about two years ago. At that time, *Poetry Events* emerged, opening a new terrain for experimentation. Left somewhat by the wayside were figures like Allen Ginsberg—who has just published a new book that went unnoticed—and the most independent writers even began to move beyond a certain subjugation to the aesthetics of Frank O'Hara, John Ashbery and Kenneth Koch (New York School), despite their being considered teachers or perhaps indirect inspirations for the current explosions of personality.

I'd now like to describe or recount some concrete events that took place here and that seem to me to be of importance for the new literature. First, a series of *Central Park Poetry Events* run by nine important poets, held in September, over the course of three afternoons in Central Park. Vito Hannibal Acconci, literature professor and admirer of Marcelin Pleynet, affixed ten sheets of legal-size paper with several typewritten lines on them to the back of the stage that opened out to the viewers in a circular fashion. *A performer* would approach each of the sheets and gesture toward them with a pointer, as the reading of certain texts (supposedly the same ones) began to be audible through the speakers. These readings were done by other performers who were located on different steps on the stairs to the left of the stage. Each of the performers on the stairs would read one line from the paper in their hands, and they would pass the microphone up and down from one to the other. The texts were very intelligent and cold. The performer moving from left to right pointing at the texts traced a horizontal movement across the entire stage, while the performers passing the microphone up and down the stairs drew a vertical line with it. These two singular dramatic actions—with the ten small sheets of paper at the back of the stage as the only scenery—together formed a quite original kind of theater. The entire *Event* constituted a refined and exacting work, designed for thinking (about, for example, reading, with its demand for horizontal movement from left to right to read a line, and up and down to move from one line of the text to the next; this poetic event alluded to all of this).

For her part, Hannah Weiner had a navy signal specialist spell out poems made of brief phrases, generally one word, using his flags. A voice would translate these poems into English, as of course the audience had not understood the poems initially. The contrast between the brief English versions and the long, colorful versions made of signal flags codes was remarkable. The "reading" ended with the launching of several flares used to transmit calls for help or to indicate one's whereabouts on the high seas; the flares burnt up above the spectators' heads.

As for William Burroughs, in an unexpected change from his usual topics, he sent a tape recording from the famous unrest in Chicago that ended up being quite interesting, although it was not clearly understood as a literary work (it seemed more a question of his having sent out, as a substitution for an actual literary work, a work of testimony—because of the proximity of the events to which the tape referred and the need for moral condemnation of them— rather than understanding as a literary work a body of writing with the structure and vocabulary of testimony).

Emmett Williams, known among other things for his poems made with computers, read poetry seated at a desk before the audience, while several *performers* piled boxes in front of him until they had completely hidden him from the spectators' view.

John Perreault "wrote" on three screens, using three slide projectors that displayed sentences at a rate of one word per slide every 30 seconds; the sentences had to do with the landscape surrounding the audience, and the words reached their eyes in temporal succession, in the same way that oral language reaches the ear. To understand these sentences, the spectator needed to follow just one of the screens, without becoming distracted by the others. The same was true with regard to the three speakers that were playing recorded material from different angles at the site.

John Giorno brought to the stage a kind of complicated stoplight with many lights that would turn on and off in accordance with the sonic oscillations of a tape recording that played the voices of the author and other people, as he burned a strange strawberry incense which filled the air with its disgustingly sweet-scented smoke.

Anne Waldman's *Event* consisted of inserting words and phrases into the middle of music made by a rock and roll band, with a microphone that she would bring to her mouth every now and then. I've intentionally left her for the end of this list, in order to link her piece with another that she created approximately a month later at the Sailors' Monument on Riverside Drive; this diachronic information will be useful for outlining a model of the tactics followed here in regard to repetitions, the originality of different works presented to the public, and the frequency of presentations. Indeed, the custom for all poets right now in New York seems to be not to turn down any possibility of appearing in public; given the large amount of activity taking place, this often forces them to repeat the same pieces or to repeat them with tiny variations. This adds a special quality to this activity: the evolution of each author can be seen very clearly. The different Poetry Readings, *Poetry Events*, etc. become time spent in a laboratory in which new possibilities for art are being destroyed or invented in a highly public way. Behind-the-scenes *"back stage"* work and rehearsals have practically been done away with, or, to put it more precisely, have been equated with public presentations and have been subsumed within them. Right now, the entire literary scene is an especially captivating *show* for anyone who is interested in the study of processes.

Returning to Anne, the second version of her *Poetry Event* consisted of a party or literary dance. With a rock and roll band placed in a kind of rotunda that also functioned as a dance floor and the author intermingling with the band members, the audience—made up almost entirely of people she knew—was invited to dance. Anne's words or poems ("*I am—I am—I am—I am*," and others that confirmed her existence for us in a similar way) mixed with the music and, just as the music did, dictated our movements ("*Come-come-come, dance-dance*," "*You are moving in the air, you are moving in the air*"). The *Event* thus turned into a party, although this party was not a real party, but rather a fictional party. Some details let the invitees in on this fact: the unsuitable space, the announcement we'd all read and that predisposed us to expect poetry, the writer's aforementioned modest innovation of appearing with the band and sending us her words from that space. In short, the entertainment ended up being unusually refined for those of us who enjoy that ambiguity, and it brought together all the virtues of a gathering for literature and a party for amusement, confirmation of friendship, relaxation. Anne Waldman is in charge of organizing poetry readings at St. Mark's Church and, at very young age (23), she is in possession of all the social, mental, and physical conditions for becoming a great writer; she has already mastered—with an implacable gentleness—the smallest movements of this world to which she is devoting all her energy.

Another literary woman who must be considered if we are to understand New York is Hannah Weiner. In November, she organized an afternoon of *Tiny Events* performed by poets at a great artists' café; it ended up being quite different from the usual kind of event, and was attended by a substantial audience, with abundant commentary in the newspapers. Some of the participants were the same ones from Central Park, and there were several additional names, among them my own. Jack Anderson performed the first poem with mirrors, reading his work *Feelings*, referring to feelings of self-esteem and love, from a sheet of paper affixed to the back of a mirror, as he circulated through the audience, putting this mirror up to their faces so that they would see the poem illustrated with their own image. I presented my work of fashion-fiction that I created in Buenos Aires with Juan Risuleo, María Larreta (model), Rivas and Alvarado (photos) and Dante Niro (objects). Jackson Mac Low unwrapped and then re-wrapped, in front of the audience, a roll of cloth that had a large number one written on it; the performance took two minutes (one for each operation). Bici Hendricks distributed to the audience several small plastic capsules—

of the sort used to package medicine—containing lines from a long poem that would in this way be distributed among all the individual consciousnesses of those present, without having ever been entirely understood except, perhaps, by the author. Carol Bergé asked questions and her small son provided not-very-understandable answers; they were positioned on opposite ends of the room in such a way that their stammering, full of affection, traversed the audience before reaching the other person. Lewis Warsh and Anne Waldman (who are married) collaborated on their *Event* titled *Home Life*: they turned on their color television, lay down on the floor, put on a recorder that repeated their own poems, *"and they turned on in the middle of the audience."* Michael Benedikt put some glossy paper tears on Carolee Schneemann's face, which had been specially made up. Hannah Weiner decoded and then performed a message that some ribbon designer had written, without knowing it, with the international code of signals (*Mike, Zulu, Whisky, Tango*) on thousands of meters of ribbon easy to obtain in the U.S.A.

I hope this deluge of information is enough to provide an idea of the adventures that are of interest to the avant-garde right now. Nevertheless, the activity that could be considered traditional (publishing journals and books) is not in the least neglected. The following journals, all of them very good, should be taken into account: *The World, Angel Hair, O to 9, Reindeer, Bones, Extensions*, all of them published informally. These have substantially filled the void left by *Mother* (edited by Peter Schjeldahl) and *Kulchur*, published by Lita Hornick, who has recently put her ability to detect the avant-garde at the service of her art collection (an incredible portrait of her is provided by her several paintings made by Warhol, an excellent Frank Stella, an excellent recent D'Arcangelo, excellent works by Robert Smithson, Ellsworth Kelly, Al Held, etc., etc.). In regards to books, the following might be at least moderately memorable: *Moving Through Air* (Lewis Warsh), *Poems* (John Giorno), *Bean Spasms* (Ted Berrigan and Ron Padgett), *Sonnets* (Ted Berrigan), *Behind the Wheel* (Michael Brownstein), *On the Wing* and *Hijacking* (Anne Waldman and Lewis Warsh, in a single volume), *RPJ Want Men* (Hannah Weiner), *Four Book* (Vito Hannibal Acconci) and *Spring in this World of Poor Mutts* (Joe Ceravolo). In terms of the somewhat older authors, an important collaboration between Robert Creeley and Robert Indiana was released: 10 silkscreen prints numbered by Indiana and 10 poems by Creeley, published in German and English. Two entire generations of poets attended the book launch, and we all contributed to the ritual, presided over by the physical presence of Allen Ginsberg. Of course, it was pleasant to exchange greetings with Robert Creeley, whom I had met a few years earlier in relation to the translation of his poems that I did with Madela Ezcurra.

Returning to the topic of the avant-garde, it would not be much of a risk to say that it is characterized, in all parts of the world, by entailing in a certain sense an investigation into the meaning of certain words. Those words—which are the categories that enable us to think about art (literature—novel—essay—poem—story; visual arts—painting—sculpture—mural, etc.)—have been attacked using the strategy of associating their signifiers to signifieds with which they would not usually be associated. Why call something a novel that "is not" a novel, or theatre something that is not theatre, if not to touch the inside of a word, to undercut the established relationship between a signified and signifier? And nevertheless literature has not distinguished itself with its contribution to this revolution carried out in the language of the arts. Although perhaps its contribution is somewhat hidden, or it is too obvious and generalized for us to be able to see it, and consists in inducing the other arts to concern themselves with their own verbal foundations, in extending the use of the term "language," and in introducing linguistic models into other domains. Following this argument, the other arts would take up the perhaps doubtful privilege of the physical realization of works that will serve to justify a transformation in the reach of certain words.

But up until now, I have referred to a generation of writers, and excluded the critics among them. However, the critics no longer think of themselves as all that different from writers who create works of fiction, and many of them are intensely active in both fields. In a gathering at the end of December organized by Nicolas Calas, in his home, with original works by Max Ernst, Miró, etc., this intelligent critic, who primarily worked on issues of surrealism and pop art, brought together an important group of critics. Among them were Rosalind Constable (*New York Magazine* and until recently the author of the secret "Executive's Newsletter" for the managers of *Time*, *Life* and *Fortune*), John Perreault (*Village Voice*), Gregory Battcock (*New York Free Press*, several anthologies, and a crucial book, *The New*

American Cinema) and several others. For us, it is important to figure out what their ideas about art in South America might be. Battcock was specifically interested in information about Caracas, a city he would soon visit, and thus he was left in my care. I talked to him about Clara Sujo, whose *Estudio Actual* [Contemporary Studio] had opened at the end of 1968; everyone who traveled through Venezuela was quite excited about it (she holds exclusive rights to Marcel Duchamp, Denis René's mobiles and other prominent works of contemporary art). I am sure that Clara Sujo would help him to define his vague idea of what's happening in the southern part of the continent, and meanwhile he'll be invited to meet some of the Argentines who are helping to create the animated artistic life of New York City: Alcides Lanza, Luis Alberto and Haru Wells (who arrived from London a year ago), Susana and Alejandro Puente, Alfredo Rodríguez Arias and his group, who just found success with *Dracula*, and many others I can't recall now.

Useful Art Manifesto (1969)

Handed out at the original performance of Street Works I *on March 15, 1969 and then partially quoted in John Perreault, "Art on the Street,"* The Village Voice *(27 March 1969), 17; first published in Collischan and Perreault, eds.,* In Plain Sight. *The typescript is titled "Street Works."*

On March 15, 1969, Eduardo Costa introduced the initial two works in his series "Useful Art Works," as part of *Street Works* performed in N.Y.C. by a group of artists and poets.

The first of these works consisted of buying at his own expense and placing in the right place the missing metal street signs at the North East corners of 42nd St. and Madison Ave., 51st St. and Fifth Ave., 49th St. and Fifth Ave., 45th St. and Fifth Ave., 44th St. and Fifth Ave., and 51st St. and Sixth Ave. These new ones replaced only some of the street signs missing in the area of midtown New York designated for the performance of *Street Works*. The signs read E 42 St, E 51 St, E 49 St, E 45 St, E 44 St, and W 51 St, and might be considered as a discontinuous literary work with six lines.

The second *Useful Art Work* consisted of painting the subway station at 42nd St. and Fifth Ave. on the Flushing Line.

These art works were intended to attack the myth of the lack of utility of the arts, while being in themselves a modest contribution to the improvement of city living conditions.

Both *Works* were performed—with the help of Scott Burton— between 2:30 and 7:00 a.m., to avoid any problems involving the municipal laws. The second *Work* could not be finished.

Announcement of Tape Poems (1969)

Co-authored with John Perreault. Typescript dated May 1, 1969 and first published in Collischan and Perreault, eds., In Plain Sight. *The final list of poems differs from the list announced here, as does the edition size. The final version of* Tape Poems *does not include the taped introduction announced here.*

A SPECIAL OFFER FOR LIBRARIES, UNIVERSITIES, COLLECTORS AND THOSE WITH A PARTICULAR INTEREST IN NEW POETRY:

Tape Poems, edited by Eduardo Costa and John Perreault, is an anthology of new works created especially for stereo tape. Most of these works do not—and cannot—exist on the printed page. They only exist as sound. They take full advantage of sound direction, pitch, volume, movement through space, sound coloration and other possibilities of stereo tape engineering.

The works in this anthology—some of which will undoubtedly turn out to be the masterpieces of this new medium—use aleatory and Found Poetry techniques, collage, literalism, conceptual approaches, autobiography, eroticism, simultaneity, and antiphony.

Many poets have already been recorded reading from their own works. *Tape Poems*, however, is not an anthology of poets reading from their written works. It is a collection of works designed for a particular medium: stereophonic tape recording. The fourteen contributors to *Tape Poems* already have considerable reputations for being in the vanguard of the new poetry. *Tape Poems* also includes a taped introduction by Eduardo Costa and John Perreault which explores some of the theoretical and aesthetic aspects of these new works and of this new medium.

The poets and their works presented in *Tape Poems* are:

1. Vito Hannibal Acconci, "Untitled"
2. Michael Benedikt, "Some Litanies"
3. Scott Burton, "Adding 'Minutes'"
4. Ted Castle & Leandro Katz, "Some Toast and Principles or Something"
5. Joseph Ceravolo, "Poems and Background"
6. Eduardo Costa, "Four Works"
7. John Giorno, "Give It To Me, Baby"
8. Dan Graham, "'Foams' plus Fill"
9. Bernadette Mayer, "The Complete Works of Anton Webern, A Movie"
10. John Perreault, "8 Works for Tape Recorder," "100 Feet of Silence and/or Intermission and/or Tape Poem to be Read from Tape, and/or etc."
11. Anne Waldman, "Six Minutes of Life"
12. Lewis Warsh, "Halloween"
13. Hannah Weiner, "Four Poems"

Tape Poems is now being offered in a first edition of 300 copies, 100 of which are signed and numbered by the editors. Order your copy of this collector's item now and receive one of the first 100 copies for the price of $15.00. Checks should be made out to Eduardo Costa and all orders sent to Tape Poems c/o Costa, 46 Grand St., N.Y.C.

An Introduction to Tape Poems (1969)

Co-authored with John Perreault. First printed on the cover of Tape Poems. *In addition to Costa's works,* Tape Poems *includes sound works by Vito Hannibal Acconci, Michael Benedikt, Scott Burton, Ted Castle and Leandro Katz, John Giorno, Joseph Ceravolo, Dan Graham, Bernadette Mayer, John Perreault, Anne Waldmann, Lewis Warsh and Hannah Weiner. The cover of* Tape Poems *has the following header: "An Introduction to* Tape Poems—*First Publication (500 copies) of Works Created Specifically for Tape." Of the originally planned 500 copies, only 30 were made.*

This is the first collection and the first "publication" of works created specifically for stereophonic tape. The works exist completely in terms of aural phenomenon, rather than in terms of visual systems of signs, thus beginning a new art of the tape recorder that has in common with written literature the fact that it refers to real language.

Some poets have already issued phonograph recordings of readings from their written works. *Tape Poems*, however, do not exist as printed works. Also there are many differences between phonograph recordings and tape recordings. Among other things, a tape recording can be easily erased, edited, and re-recorded.

We see *Tape Poems* as the initial exploration of a new medium for the artistic use of language that will co-exist with written literature.

The use of this new medium will call attention to ordinary speech as one of the most important ways of producing aesthetic emotion through language. It will regain for "literature" tones of voice, pitch, and the other characteristics of spoken language that are lost when it is translated into the printed word. These nuances are linguistically relevant, since they can indicate age, sex, class, geographical origin and emotional state of the speaker.

Written literature can be thought of as consisting of some of the possible combinations of the letters of the alphabet arranged on a plane; but aural literature, such as *Tape Poems*, consists of sounds arranged in space.

Another difference between aural literature and written literature is that in written literature the author has little control over the speed at which his language is perceived, whereas in aural literature—as in the cinema—the author does have control.

In the past, documentation was restricted to writing. Now as well as writing we use photography and tape recording to document and to remember. Tape recordings have become sound snapshots.

But there is a difference between photo documentation and sound documentation. In a photograph the materiality is not the same as the materiality of the object represented. For instance, a photo of a person is not flesh, but paper. But when we play a tape we have sound as in the original phonic language.

Of course, the fact that the materiality is the same does not mean that when we listen to a tape-recording of language we are listening to the real language. We are only in front of language mediated through a different system of restrictions, through another code than that of written language.

The tape recorder is already as necessary as the typewriter. It may soon replace it. In the future it may not be necessary to learn to read and write. Perhaps all we will need to know is how to hold a microphone and push a few buttons.

Four Works: First Tale, Second Tale, and Third Tale (1969)

Transcription of works included in Tape Poems. *In "First Tale," the voice is deep and slow and seems masculine, but gradually changes so that, at the end, it corresponds to the listener's expectations of what an adult woman's voice sounds like; "First Tale" uses text from two short articles on page 49 of the June 21, 1968 issue of* Time, *titled "Upholding Aid to Students" and "Approval to 'Stop & Frisk.'" In "Second Tale," the voice is altered in the beginning to make it sound as if a child were reading the news; the voice changes gradually so that, by the end, it sounds like an adult woman's voice; "Second Tale" uses two other articles from the same issue of* Time, *"Ultimatum to Nuns" and "Explorer of the Bloodstream," from page 73 and 71. The first work is the first tale; the second work is the second tale; the third work is both tales listened to simultaneously; and the fourth work is "Property Poem," the next text in this volume.*

Instructions: Please notice the number on the counter of your tape recorder. Then listen to the left track by itself, and once the poem called "First Tale" is finished, go back to the number your counter is indicating now and listen to the right track by itself. After "Second Tale," please turn on both tracks.

First Tale: In skirt and blouse? Yes, decided Los Angeles' progressive-minded Sisters of the Immaculate Heart of Mary, who last fall made a number of reforms in their way of life, including the right to wear civilian dress. Scientists have long known that hemoglobin in the bloodstream carries oxygen from the lungs to the body tissues and returns waste products from the tissues to be inhaled from the lungs. But not until Perutz learned how to put the pieces of his intricate puzzle together did anyone begin to understand just how hemoglobin does its job. Each hemoglobin molecule, Perutz found, consists of 10,000 atoms, of which four are iron atoms that have an affinity for oxygen. In the lungs, in the presence of oxygen, the hemoglobin molecule changes shape, moving each of the four iron atoms, which are located in separate "pockets" on its surface, to different positions. This change increases by 300 times the molecule's attraction for oxygen atoms, pulling four of them into combination with the iron atoms. It is only because there are 280 million hemoglobin molecules in each red corpuscle.

Second Tale: Members of the Board of Education for both Rensselaer and Columbia counties argued that such programs violate the First Amendment ban on "establishment of religion." Last week the court upheld the state. New York's law, it said, was an aid to children, not religion. In 1947, the court had ruled that states could reimburse parents for the cost of bussing their children to parochial schools, and Justice Byron White's majority opinion relied heavily on that earlier case. "Of course," he agreed, "books are different from buses." But in this case they are no more of a threat to the Constitution. The public school board must find that they are secular, thus answering the objection that the state might be supplying religious books. Pointing out parenthetically that many apparently secular books may be religious in their treatment of such subjects as evolution, the three dissenters, Justices Douglas, Fortas and Black, all heatedly argued that the First Amendment's rule was being badly compromised. Said Black: "It requires no prophet to foresee that on the argument used to support this law others could be upheld providing for funds to buy property on which to erect religious school buildings, to pay the salaries of religious school teachers, and finally to pick up all the bills for religious schools. I still subscribe to the belief that tax-raised funds cannot constitutionally be used to support religious schools, even to the extent of one penny." Approval to stop and frisk. It happens almost every day: a policeman catches sight of a suspicious character, stops him and frisks him. But doesn't the Fourth Amendment specifically bar "unreasonable searches and seizures?" It does indeed, said the Supreme Court last week, but the operative word is "unreasonable." Speaking for an 8-to-1 majority, Chief Justice Warren held that the Constitution permits a policeman to accost an individual if there is good reason to suspect that he is up to no good, and to search him for weapons if there is good reason to suspect that he may be armed.

Explanation: In the last two pieces, the changes on the voice tones are narrating a certain reality. First, a change of sex and then a change of age are told to us irregardless of what the speakers say. The information contained in certain parameters of the human voice tells us, usually, about these realities, and that information is immediately and not very consciously understood or decoded in our everyday life.

Four Works: Property Poem (1969)

Transcription of work included in Tape Poems.

This tape belongs to: Record your name here after erasing this instruction.
Address: Record address after erasing instruction.
Phone number: Record number after erasing instruction.

Proposal for a Street Work (1969)

Published in Collischan and Perreault, eds., In Plain Sight. *This is a proposal for the* Street Works IV *exhibition at the Architectural League of New York, which was a series of events that took place between October 2 and 25, 1969. The exhibition was organized by John Perreault, Marjorie Strider, and Hannah Weiner; participating artists were Vito Acconci, Arakawa, Scott Burton, Costa, Les Levine, Abraham Lubelski, Bernadette Mayer, John Perreault, Marjorie Strider, and Hannah Weiner. This proposal was rejected, and Costa proposed* 1000 Street Works, *the next text.*

To tear a page of a book from the Architectural League Library—eventually donated by the author of this project. To write on the bottom of the preceding page (if the torn page is, for instance, page 48) "continued on page 48." To enlarge torn page 48/49 to poster size, keeping its original typography, shape, etc. To print in the top left corner of the page "continued from page 47, *The Art of the Middle Ages,* A. League Library No. 3582R" and in the bottom right corner of the page "continued on page 50 Idem liber." To paste at least about 100 copies of enlarged page 48/49 all around the area designated for the Street Works. To print in the top left side of page 50 of the same book "continued from page 49."

In case there isn't a Library in the Architectural League, the same thing could be done with any book or magazine inside the building, indicating its specific location on the enlarged pasted-on-the-street page.

1000 STREET WORKS (1969)

Published in Collischan and Perreault, eds., In Plain Sight. See note for previous text for more information. The passage in square brackets is scribbled out in the typescript; the phrase "pieces of art" in parentheses was typed in above "objects." The program for Street Works IV *announces that on the opening night of the exhibition, October 2, Costa would "place 25 'art works' unidentifiable as such on the street" and that, between October 3 and 25, Costa "will place 1000 'art works' unidentifiable as such on the street."*

From October 2 to 25, 1969, I will place in locations from 60th to 70th Streets between 5th Ave. and Lexington 1000 different art works that will not be identified as such by a signature or any other indication of their culturally conventional nature.

These works are intended to be charged with the implications that art may have for the person who passes by and notices them as such, and collected or just remembered by that person.

[Because nobody will pay to make these objects (pieces of art) his own and some messages might be received by the art audience from non-art objects in the streets, and there will be no way of telling if the works have really been made, these *1000 Street Works* become a commentary on some conventions of art history and economics as well as a way of questioning the present of the arts, and my contribution to *Street Works* remains perhaps mostly a literary one.]

Some of these art works will cost nothing while others (because of the materials involved) will cost me up to 15 dollars. Some of them can be picked up and kept, while some others can only be remembered and will perhaps stay adhered to the walls, pavement, trees, etc. after Oct. 25.

Photographers or columnists who may be interested in keeping records of this experience are invited to walk the indicated area and describe by means of words and photographs the works they may find.

A FASHION (A TALE) (1970)

Co-authored with Juan Risuleo. First published as "Una moda (relato)" in the Mexican magazine Caballero: Revista masculina *(February 1970). These texts accompany photos of a model wearing the items described. These are the credits listed in the magazine: "Ideas and Text: Eduardo Costa, Juan Risuleo; Photos: Humberto Rivas, Roberto Alvarado; Model: María Larreta; Creation of the Objects for the Photos: Dante Niro."*

FOR GRAND PARTIES OR CASUAL WEAR. These rings or useless thimbles completely encase the tip of a finger selected at random, or two or three on one hand.

They envelop the finger from the middle joint onwards, including the nail to the very tip. If the nail is very long, it creates a truly interesting effect.

A SKIN OF GOLD OVER NATURAL SKIN. This season we present earrings made of a thin film of gold covering practically the entirety of the model's ear, conforming to its every minute curve, all of the details and accidents of its shape. These pieces—simple yet sophisticated, classic in their effect yet quite innovative—must be custom-made, taken from a mold that is an exact copy of the very ear they are designed to encase.

A variation for elegant ladies who enjoy—and who doesn't?—an exotic touch for exotic occasions: earrings that encase the ear in all its details, curves, expanse, etc. while also featuring a earlobe elongated downwards in the style of certain ancient Indian icons.

REAL HAIR OF GOLD. As part of this same line, we are presenting these strands to be worn interlaced in your natural hair. Our designer appears to have translated a classical image from the world of poetry to create this astonishing jewelry. Interlace into your own hair—whether light or dark—these 24 carat gold strands, in a set of either four or five. A light clasp at one of the ends will enable you to securely fasten them to the rest of your hair.

As some of the ladies—and gentlemen—reading this have probably guessed by now, we have also envisioned a use for these rings on the toes, in which case they would cover the toe entirely and not just the last two joints. These rings have been designed with their concealment in mind, since, obviously, if shoes are worn, they are rendered invisible.

Another variation requires an ear that still retains the piercing done occasionally on newborn girls; the earring that will envelop the ear will also incorporate that hole, through which a hoop earring can be supported as it traditionally would be.

"There is no more aesthetic contemplation because aesthetics is dissolving itself into social life."
– Octavio Paz

LETTER TO ATHENA TACHA ABOUT THE *Art in the Mind* EXHIBITION (1970)

Letter from the archive of Athena Tacha. This is Costa's response to a letter from Athena T. Spear (now Athena Tacha) soliciting submissions for Art in the Mind, *which she curated for the Allen Art Museum at Oberlin College from April 17 to May 12, 1970. Tacha rejected Costa's proposal, and he instead submitted the next text, the work titled* A piece that is… *The name of the fashion designer Costa mentions has been replaced by the generic term "fashion designer."*

Dear Mrs. Spear:

Thank you for your letter from Jan. 30. I've been thinking about the material to send you. In this moment I would like very much to show my "conceptual" jewelry. This consists of, for instance, a ring of conventional shape on which a big precious stone has been set: but the whole ring is totally covered by a thin film of 24 kts. (pure) gold. Through the gold the shape of the stone facets, as well as all details of the setting and rest of the ring, are exposed. A brief caption (which actually "makes" the piece and because of which it can be considered conceptual) spells "Platinum and 4 kts. diamond, covered by pure yellow gold." Also the price can be added, like in some store displays: "$3500." It will not be made clear if such is the price of the real diamond ring or of the art work consisting of the fiction of a nonexistent platinum and diamond ring, hidden by real gold.

A while ago I made a literary piece which was the description of some pure gold jewelry which consisted of a thin film of gold covering parts of the human body. The earrings were made of the ear cast of the person who was going to wear it, the ring from the finger cast, and so on. I enclose something people from *Vogue* made out of my descriptions of nonexistent jewelry. Close to the Avedon photograph of the earring you will find an explanation in which they did what they could to understand the work, and they asked for Alloway's help (He told me they also changed what he said about it). After *Vogue's* and other publicity given to this fashion-fiction work here and in Europe, it was imitated and actually made, first in Germany and then in Paris, by [a fashion designer], which I consider the last step of my piece, the one which closes it. I could send you all the documentation concerning this piece if you wanted to show it: 1) my fashion-fiction texts; 2) what *Vogue* made of them; 3) other articles and photos—*Chicago Tribune, Der Spiegel, Status,* etc.; 4) the media version of [the fashion designer's] imitation. But the whole thing is already somehow known here, and I would rather show this new piece I described above.

Please let me know what you think. Also, may I suggest that you write to Scott Burton, 86 Thompson St., NY, NY 10012? He's done many conceptual art works and written—among other related articles—the introduction to the catalogue *Live in your head—When attitudes become form.*

Sincerely yours,
Eduardo Costa

A PIECE THAT IS ESSENTIALLY THE SAME AS A PIECE MADE BY ANY OF THE FIRST CONCEPTUAL ARTISTS, DATED TWO YEARS EARLIER THAN THE ORIGINAL AND SIGNED BY SOMEBODY ELSE (1970)

First published in Athena T. Spear, ed., Art in the Mind *(Oberlin OH: Allen Art Museum, 1970), u.p.*

A piece that is essentially the same as a piece made by any of the first conceptual artists, dated two years earlier than the original and signed by somebody else.

EDUARDO COSTA
January 1970

You See a Dress (1970)

Transcribed from a digital recording. Performed at the Wadsworth Atheneum on April 14, 1970 as part of Four Theater Pieces, *curated by Scott Burton; the other performers were Vito Acconci, Scott Burton, and John Perreault. The program included this text by Costa: "My piece does not imply a strong belief in the importance of physical objects or in the importance of visual over other kinds of perception. Also, it brings theatre closer to Hypnotism and Fashion."*

Soon the third piece in this program will begin. Soon the third piece in this program will begin.

You start returning from the lobby. You start returning from the lobby, walking towards your seat. You spot your seat. You say some last words. After the break, you produce some final sounds by walking and moving the seat. Soft sounds of feet stepping on the carpet. Low coughs. The last words mumbled, mixed with the voice in this tape.

You sit down. You put out your cigarettes. This takes a few seconds, perhaps one minute. You start paying attention to this tape. You shut up. You listen to it.

Two or three of you come in late. Those who have stopped in the ladies' or men's rooms are enjoying the last puffs on your cigarettes outside.

You are sitting down. You feel comfortable. You relax. You develop a certain feeling of expectation.

First act.

Now you close your eyes. Now you close your eyes. Close your eyes. You recline, leaning comfortably against the back of your seat. You close your eyes. You relax. You relax. You keep your eyes closed. You start hearing the music. You start hearing the music. It is a soft symphony.

It is a romantic symphony you think you have heard before. You know. You remember the name of the symphony. You will soon recall it. The music is the only presence on the stage, coming out from the stage and invading your mind. You let the music take over your mind, making you feel even more relaxed and comfortable. You keep your eyes closed. You relax.

The main character of the play comes in. It is an extremely attractive girl. You think her face looks somehow like a girl's face you've seen recently. Your gaze follows her form. The form of the character she plays. You keep your eyes closed. She has long hair falling down her shoulders, a provocative smile, long flexible neck, slim tall body. You look again. You notice the rich elegant dress, a sort of black silk tunic that falls down touching the floor. She is there, in front of you, inside you, here, in this place. She's as much yours as anything you touch, anything you see. For a while, you see her standing, floating, still, before you. The music keeps playing. You see now the relationship between the music and the only character. Sometimes the music and the girl complement, sometimes they counteract, they fight each other. You like that. You like it. You groove on it for a while. You keep your eyes closed. You wonder what's going to happen next. Then you see the girl coming closer to the audience, becoming bigger as she approaches you as much as possible. You see her slowly, maliciously unbuttoning her tunic. You foresee nudity. Nudity, you think again. The body, you think again. A value in itself. But still you feel thrilled, a little uncertain. The female body, you think, the female body. You experience suspense. Then, suddenly, you see the falling silk rolled on the floor around the feet of the young lady, who's let it fall with a quick movement of her shoulders. You breathe. You feel relieved, and also you feel frustrated, uneasy. She is not naked. Under her tunic, she was not hiding just her body, but another outfit. You hesitate. You look at her again. It takes you a few seconds to understand. It is not a girl. It is a female impersonator, you realize, wearing an attractive outfit. The outfit consists of a blouse to which two transparent plastic breasts have been added. You see the beautiful feminine breasts through which you see also the boyish flat chest of the impersonator. But this is not all. The outfit is continued by a pair of pants, the fabric of which follows like a second skin every detail of the shape of the sex of the boy, totally exposing his testicles and prick.

Evolution of the Wheel and Spiral Motifs in the Work of Marcel Duchamp (1977/2009)

Typescript titled "Evolución de los motivos 'rueda' y 'espiral' en la obra de Marcel Duchamp." The typescript includes small illustrations of Duchamp's works and concludes with the following note, which links Costa's investigation of the wheel and spiral motifs in Duchamp to two Costa works: "A panel similar to this text was exhibited along with The Duchamp-Costa Wheel *in* Homage to Marcel Duchamp, Galería Arte Nuevo, Buenos Aires, 1977. *At that time, the bicycle did not yet exist, as it is from 1979–80 and has been exhibited only as a model in* Eminent Immigrants, Snug Harbor Cultural Center, NY (c. 1985). *In 2008,* The Duchamp/Costa Bicycle *was exhibited as an installation of 30 similar bicycles at the Jumex Foundation/Collection, Mexico City, as part of the exhibition* The (Unruly) History of the Readymade, *curated by Jessica Morgan. In 2009, it was exhibited as an installation/performance at the Buenos Aires art fair ArteBA, where the public participated in the exhibition, riding the bicycles on a track designed as part of the floor."*

1. In 1904-5, at the age of 17, Marcel made a small drawing, *Sharpening Machine*. A wheel—though without spokes, forming part of the machine portrayed—occupies a central place in the composition.
2. In a 1909 drawing, we see two spirals that face one another, forming an element of the balustrade on which the characters lean. It is called *At the Palais de Glace*, and presents the spiral for the first time in Duchamp's work as a decorative motif. The drawing next to it is a similar example.
3. *Sundays* is an ink drawing from 1909 that depicts wheels with spokes, in this case part of a baby carriage. Above the wheels, we see the spirals that have the usual function of shock absorbers. For the first time, Duchamp clearly represents the

classic wheel and spiral "collaborating" to make a machine work.

4. In subsequent years, Marcel became interested in painting nudes, family scenes, some landscapes. The wheel no longer appears as a motif, but in contrast often governs the composition of the painting, which is radial. *Sonata*, depicting his mother and sisters during a musical recital at home, is a good example of this.

5. *Chocolate Grinder*, 1913, depicts another machine, with rotating cylinders in the shape of an enlarged wheel.

6. With *Bicycle Wheel*, an "imaginative leap" is made. The wheel moves from being a motif to being the central topic, and from representation to real object. It is the first (assisted) "ready-made."

7. The *Bottle Dryer*, another ready-made, is a device made of a number of circular rings with bent points at their ends, so we're able to insert the necks of bottles onto them. Each ring is a version of the visual sign "wheel," the spokes of which would be external to the outer circumference of a common wheel.

8. In *With Hidden Noise*, the ball of twine between two metal sheets joined to one another by four screws is to the spiral motif what the bicycle wheel is to the "wheel" motif. It is called *With Hidden Noise* because of an object located inside the ball of twine that makes noise when shaken, but what is interesting for our analysis is that it presents a "ready made" version of the common spiral (ball) and of the helicoid (screw threads).

9. *To Be Looked at (from the Other Side of the Glass) with One Eye, Up Close, for Almost an Hour* is an oil painting (with other materials) on glass that Duchamp made in Buenos Aires. The obelisk rests on what we might consider an abstract wheel—that is, no longer a wheel with spokes, but rather a circumference with radii. This work illustrates the second important leap in the evolution of the wheel motif in Duchamp's work.

10. In 1918, as he left for Buenos Aires, Marcel drew a map of the Americas for a friend of his. *Farewell to Florine* depicts a question mark above Buenos Aires with the spiral abnormally accentuated.

11. Upon his return to New York, Duchamp finished *The Large Glass*, painting these variations on abstract wheels (one concentric circle and two circles with external radii) that date from 1920–1921.

12. *Rotary Demisphere (Precision Optics)*, 1925, is a machine whose subject matter is the visual sign of the wheel in one of its abstract iterations. In *Rotary…* the wheels do not move a machine, serving an ulterior motive, but rather the machine moves a wheel, in service to it. The wheel and the spiral appear solidly and originally conjoined, forming a machine like the baby carriage from 1909, although obviously quite different.

13. In 1935 at a Paris inventors' fair, Duchamp presented discs that produced, when spun on the turntable of a record player, optical effects with blue and red spiral and circular shapes on a black or white background. The *Rotoreliefs* are a testimony to the artist's intent to introduce this new form of alliance between wheel and spiral into the circuit of his inventions.

An analysis of the wheel and the spiral in Duchamp's work suggests that, had he continued to develop his own creative model, Marcel would have invented a new wheel, and subsequently a new bicycle. This new wheel (with many possible practical applications and symbolic meanings) would have just one spoke in the shape of a spiral instead of normal spokes. It has been said that the spokes of a wheel express the relationship between its fixed center and its mobile circumference (Cirlot); we might also say that in this case the spiral expresses that same relationship, and additionally assures its elasticity. In other words, we would be faced with an invention that includes a machine's shock absorption within its wheels, instead of constituting it in the form of an element entailing a separate solution (see Duchamp/Costa Wheel *model).*

DUCHAMP: THE BATHTUB OR AN ASSISTED MURAL "READY-MADE" (1977)

First published as "Duchamp: La Bañadera o un 'Ready-Made' Mural," with illustrations, in the cultural section of the Argentine newspaper La Opinión, *18 September 1977, 10–11 and then in* Revista de la Universidad de México *37.8 (December 1981), 25–28. Costa added the term "assisted" to the title for the present volume.*

If one were to provide a comprehensive description of the manifold work of Marcel Duchamp, we would clearly see in it the emergence of op art, conceptual art, body art, happenings, a number of literary tendencies, the idea of chance arrangements in modern music, and above all a spirit of free inventiveness and aesthetic seriousness that imbues the few interesting works of this century's European and American avant-gardes. Nevertheless, Duchamp's oeuvre has not yet been decoded, and many doubt the possibility of completing this task. From my perspective, I believe that this desire shared by legions of critics and artists is slowly being realized, and that two or three memorable attempts (I'll speak about one of them later on) point to a way forward, covering much of the necessary ground.

But in addition to exegetists, Marcel has a legion of people who know his thinking well and transmit it (in this case his thinking is almost the same thing as his work), as they are captivated by its simple and enduring charm. One of them, in Buenos Aires, is Juan Esteban Fassio, my first teacher on Duchamp. In the library-bedroom-dining-room of his house in the Once neighborhood, Esteban initiated us, two or three spontaneous disciples, with a reading of *The Green Box*, that box-book in which Duchamp reproduced the notes he had been writing for more than ten years, based on *The Large Glass*. And, as if to highlight his gift of knowledge with an object more memorable than words, he gave me a reproduction of *Nude Descending a Staircase.*

Some five years later in 1966, I met Octavio Paz and similarly, with him, I developed that kind of instant relationship that joins natural teachers to their students. Octavio also entrusted a number of precious words to my more or less awakened mind, and among them were some in reference to Duchamp. Two years later—the same year as Marcel's death—I received a copy of Paz's book *Marcel Duchamp* in the mail.

Marcel and Octavio had known each other quite well and one visible result of their friendship is this extraordinary book-box that compiles the most intelligent interpretations with the most complete documentary material—including a reproduction of *The Bride Stripped Bare by Her Bachelors, Even*; what's more, the image is reprinted on transparent plastic. But I especially admired Paz's essay "The Castle of Purity," which is included in the book, and which gave me a glimpse into the meaning behind *The Bride...* and its elements.

In 1975, and with some knowledge of Marcel in my memory, I was invited, along with the artist Scott Burton, to have dinner in New York at the home of an old acquaintance, the art dealer Donald Droll, whose gallery owns some of Duchamp's works. Donald lives in the house where Marcel spent the last nine years of his life, so I thought to ask him if he might have left behind any traces of his time in that apartment on Tenth Street. Droll replied that there weren't any, except for a few decorated ceramic tiles that Duchamp had had placed around the bathtub. We immediately interrupted dinner and went into the bathroom. There we found a quite normal bathtub, set halfway into the floor and enclosed by three white tile walls. Six of these tiles had been replaced by ceramic tiles decorated with representations of flowers— very pretty, charming examples of folk art.

Up to this point, there was nothing special, just a bathroom fixture with some modifications made by a diligent homeowner. Nevertheless, given that we were dealing with Duchamp, his ready- mades immediately came to mind, especially *Fountain*, since both the urinal with that title and this bathtub belong to the world of the bathroom and are made of the same material (porcelain). Nevertheless, the bathtub is different from *Fountain*, not just because of its function and form, but also because it was used over the years by the artist and his family, and hence was not a new object; it was also "assisted" so as to differentiate it from the previous ready-mades, making it the only mural "ready-made." After spending some time on our memories of *Fountain*, we then recalled the bottle of perfume that Marcel labeled *Belle Haleine*, the other ready-made that belongs to the world of the bathroom, as well as his scenes of women bathing from around 1910. These precursors motivated us to continue investigating our discovery.

Looking more closely at the added ceramic tiles, we saw that at least one of the flowers depicted "was" a wheel—that is to say, it naively illustrated a classical combination that occurs, throughout the history of ornamental motifs, between wheels and flowers, especially the rose (when it is open, not as a bud, and when seen from the front). This integration of rose and wheel finds its most well known expression in the Gothic rose window. And this flower-wheel has a spiral drawn on it, which leads us to recall Marcel's second motorized machine *Rotary Demisphere*, in which various concentric circles, lightly decentered, outline the figure of a spiral inscribed between the largest and smallest circles. The flowers depicted on the other ceramic tiles can also be considered flower-wheels, in which the lines of the petals that lead from the center to the maximum circumference are the same as the spokes of a typical wheel.

In the flowers that do not feature an inscribed spiral, we see instead a series of tiny circles that proceed from largest to smallest in the corners not occupied by the leaves and buds, which are actually helicoid-spirals, probably depicting the pollen that circulates in the immediate area around a pistil. The flower in another tile also recalls the classic sewing machine wheel, with curved spokes, depicted by Duchamp in a drawing, *Mi-Carême*, from 1909.

Up until this moment, all evidence seemed to indicate that the ready-made that we had just found fit with Duchamp's visual interests and metaphysical obsessions. But in order to consider the assisted bathtub as a work with a place in the artist's production—and since it was not signed or recognized as such previously—it would have to be replicated in other versions or in different ways, existing as a realization or example of an abstract model that had to be discovered, a particular development of a motif or systematic theme in the great chess player's oeuvre. This is the reason why I dedicated myself in the following months to studying Duchamp's entire body of work, often drawing on the catalogue *Marcel Duchamp* compiled by Anne d'Harnoncourt and Kynaston McShine for the Museum of Modern Art in New York and the Philadelphia Museum of Art.

Out of this analysis the first thing that became clear was that Marcel had unconsciously developed the motifs of spiral and wheel throughout practically his entire body of work, initially as a part of ornamentations or machines, then as a structuring element of the compositions of his oil paintings that include these two forms, later in his works that were real versions of them (*Bicycle Wheel* and *With Hidden Noise*), and finally in his abstract versions. These developments are further explicated— and illustrated—in my contribution to the Buenos Aires gallery Arte Nuevo's *Homenaje a Duchamp* [*Homage to Duchamp*]. But it wasn't until the flowers that decorated his bathtub that the final development of these two forms in Duchamp's work would appear; they are examples of what we can call the visual sign "circumference with radii," which fuses the wheel versions with the flower versions, and at the same time combines this fusion with the spiral.

As I learned in subsequent months of study, the bathtub forms a natural unity with the flowers that surround it, because it is a realization or example of another of Duchamp's recurring themes, the theme of landscapes with water. Indeed, this theme is also systematic within Duchamp's body of work, and we find it for the first time in the oil painting *Landscape at Blainville*, painted when he was fifteen years old. Between this work and *Given: 1. The Waterfall, 2. The Illuminating Gas*, his last work, depicting a naked woman next to a pond, there are other versions of the theme, some represented explicitly and others concealed beneath distortions similar at times to those produced by dream work. Among the explicit depictions, in addition to the two already mentioned, we should include: 1) *Laundry Barge*, an oil painting on cardboard that depicts an artists' housing complex built along a river with a background of vegetation; 2) the ready-made *Pharmacy*, a landscape with water and flowers signed by a "bad" painter which Duchamp then also signed after adding two drops of color; 3) the pair of slides that he "assisted" in Buenos Aires, *Hand Stereoscopicon Slide*, in which two prismatic images drawn by hand by the artist on a photographic background of water and sky are joined together when viewed through a stereoscope; 4) *L.H.O.O.Q.*, the famous assisted ready-made on the *Mona Lisa* whose background is of course a landscape of mountains with water; and 5) *Moonlight on the Bay at Basswood*, a landscape featuring a forest and water painted with ink, pencil, and chocolate on blue paper.

The non-explicit depictions of the same theme are equally important, especially one that appears on numerous occasions and is illuminated by Octavio Paz's interpretation of *The Bride* and its relationship with *Given*:... Paz observes that the subject matter of both works is the mythological episode that relates the story of Diana's bath and Actaeon's destruction. In this story, the hunter Actaeon, while on a walk with his dogs, surprises a nude Diana when he happens upon the place where the goddess is bathing. Diana in turn surprises Actaeon as he is gazing upon her. She punishes him, turning him into a deer that his own dogs chase and end up devouring. Both *The Bride...* and *Given*:... show a nude woman next to a pond or lake with a background of vegetation. As I said, the subject matter is explicit in the second example and less apparent in the first, although it's possible that it's "clear" to the unconscious of many viewers.

Although we will not be able to summarize Octavio's precise and marvelous interpretation here—which can be read in his essay, * Water Writes Always in * Plural (the title is a quote from a text by Duchamp in which every instance of the English article "the" is replaced by an asterisk)—I will mention one more of his discoveries. In *Given*:..., Octavio writes, the "tub" of *The Bride...* "turns into a lake and the 'wasp-motor' into the naked girl." And although when Paz talks about the "tub" he seems to be referring to the parallelepiped in the bottom part of the work, his observation ends up being correct, as it follows, according to poetic instinct, the track left by the name "tub" and in this way arrives at the pond-lake.

The parallelepiped which can now be identified as the true "tub" or "bathtub" that according to *The Green Box* "functions in service of the hygiene of the bride" appears carefully depicted for the first time in oil on a semicircle of glass in *Glider Containing a Water Mill in Neighboring Metals*, which we must consider one of the non-explicit versions of the theme of the landscape with water. When describing this study for *The Bride...*, Duchamp said that the double wheel or water mill inside it "should be activated by a waterfall that I did not want to depict in order to avoid the trap of once again becoming a landscape painter."

I don't think it's excessive to say that the parallelepiped—which periodically shows up in Marcel's work—brings together two figurative motifs from his production: the stroller or baby carriage from his early drawings and the pond-lake from the landscapes with water. Further, this parallelepiped "is" in Duchamp's real life his own bathtub, "assisted" by the vegetation on the tiles that underscores its role as a pond or lake under a roof, with a place in every ordinary home. The waterfall that Marcel mentioned is the shower, or even the water that falls out of the faucet to fill the "pond."

I actually think that if we look at things in this way, we will see an important—and slightly startling—aspect of the updated version of the Diana myth, as proposed by Duchamp and discovered by Paz. His story narrates, on its least sophisticated level, the accidental incursion of a (male) family member into the sanctum of the bathroom, where he is surprised to find the naked body of a woman of the house, a body upon which custom does not allow him to gaze. Of course, *The Bride...* requires other simultaneous interpretations in order to exhaustively elucidate its meaning. But my aim is simply to clarify the meaning and the place of Duchamp's *Bathtub* within his body of work. And I believe that it should be considered an assisted ready-made; this work is to the representations of landscapes with water what *Bicycle Wheel* is to the many representations of the wheel, and similarly what *With Hidden Noise* with its ball of twine and its bolts is to the many representations of the ordinary spiral and helicoid. In other words, this recently discovered "ready-made" that I am venturing to title *Bathtub* provides a three-dimensional version, already made and used on a daily basis, of an element of profound, mythical presence and symbolic significance that shows up previously—and later—in Duchamp's work as distinct realizations of an abstract model, which is also present (the parallelepiped).

I would also like to note the importance of Duchamp's work for the formulation of a possible theory of the visual sign. The diachronic study of his work allows us to argue that Marcel worked unconsciously in this sense, presenting objects and representations of objects "referring" to a single abstract form, which language (that is to say its different names), its function, its materiality, etc. have accustomed us to conceive as completely different. This is despite the fact that from a visual point of view (and this should be particularly worrisome for painters) they "signify" the same thing, because they are members of the same family in terms of their image.

History of a Work of Fiction (1980s?)

Undated typescript with handwritten additions. The gallery mentioned here is the Espacio Giesso in Buenos Aires.

In 1965 I made a series of objects that had the materiality, size, and look of sophisticated jewelry. I wanted to take photographs of these objects and write some fashion copy to go with the photos so that they would be perceived as jewelry by a potential audience. I then produced a series of slides presenting the different pieces: earrings, a single strand of "hair" made of gold, rings, toe rings. They were a bit outrageous when compared to existing jewelry but a bit intelligent too—or "conceptual"—which was new in jewelry, if not in the visual arts. The set of slides together with the captions that I wrote for each photo already made a nice piece of fiction. As such they were shown— on one of those glass top cubes with light inside that we use for viewing slides—at a Buenos Aires gallery in 1966. No one thought of buying this piece, the title of which was *A Fashion*, but someone commissioned me to custom make one pair of the earrings shown. I hesitated but finally decided to do them, thinking that sometimes fiction becomes reality and that it was okay to develop this possibility of the work.

Fashion Fiction: A New Genre (1980s?)

Typescript.

I think that fashion spreads, as shown in fashion magazines, are all pieces of fiction and fantasy—sometimes even masterpieces of fiction— the function of which is to dazzle the reader with the presentation of a world where only beauty and sophistication count. To me, this function is neither regrettable nor laudable, but simply characteristic of the way in which fashion has been presented to the public through the media of magazines, newspapers, shows, etc. With this in mind, I have elaborated the idea of doing a work of fiction that has the form of a fashion spread—or an illustrated tale or poem, if you prefer to call it that—a fashion-fiction of picture and caption which will introduce non-existent (unmanufactured and, at the time of their insertion into the media, unobtainable) fashions into real life. For me, at the time of their realization, the fashion fiction will not be thought of in the usual terms of the beauty, novelty or practicality of the real objects but only in terms of how the photograph and texts will appear in the magazine. But after being inspired by my photographs and captions, someone could translate these words and pictures, these objects of fashion-fiction (or characters of my stories, if you prefer to call them that) and produce and sell real, available objects. I am especially interested in the fact that they might begin to be used, manufactured, and sold with all those necessary differences that the real material and its use in real life will impose on my fantasy.

The Shower Curtain, Even (1987)

Letter to the editor first published in The Village Voice, *22 December 1987, 58.*

Artist Victor Bouillon, in collaboration with filmmaker Susan Emerling, has pulled off a witty feat of production and reproduction: the *Large Shower Curtain*, a full-color silkscreen of Marcel Duchamp's *Large Glass* (formally titled *The Bride Stripped Bare by her Bachelors, Even*) on transparent polyvinyl. The privileged owners of this elegant shower curtain will, if they are women, be protected by the substance of the story that this curtain brings into the bathroom. Men had better be respectful if they are to approach its area of influence.

Octavio Paz's interpretation of the *Large Glass*—the best to date— suggests that it is a representation of the myth of Diana and Actaeon. In the story as told by Virgil, Diana, the goddess of chastity, is surprised while bathing in a pond by the gaze of the young hunter. She sees him seeing her and punishes the mortal by converting him into a deer that his own dogs devour.

This myth is particularly relevant to the art world because it deals with the pleasures of seeing, and its dangers. This is why it obsessed Duchamp, who used the same theme realistically in his last, and major, work, *Etant donnés*. It is also as appropriate to the bathroom as it is to Virgil's poetry or the Philadelphia Museum of Art. In our bathtub-pond we frequently reenact, with bourgeois mildness, the myth of Diana. A male of the house can, intentionally or by accident, see a naked female bather. If she sees him, she might be angered and scream, and the intruder will have to retreat in shame. Duchamp was a master of these associations, and his work commented on the continuum of the most hierarchical substance of art and its everyday incarnations.

The *Large Shower Curtain* is $80, plus $3 shipping and $6.66 tax for New York State residents (total: $89.66) from Hobbyhorse Project, P.O. Box 34, Canal Street Station, New York, N.Y. 10013-0034, 477-4191 (in New York, allow one week for delivery) and at the Museum Shop of the Philadelphia Museum of Art, a partial sponsor of the *Curtain* (which also has the approval of Teeny Duchamp herself).

Letter to Ann Gussow about Marcel Duchamp's Bathtub (1988)

Typescript.

Dear Ms. Gussow:

I am writing to you after my associate Catherine Frederick has told me that you requested some clarification on the Video we have started at your apartment (No. 2).

I first came in touch with said apartment at a party given by Mr. Droll while he was your tenant. I found the bathroom interesting as the appropriate setting for illustrating the myth of Diana as it is reenacted in the contemporary home. In the classic version Diana is the goddess of chastity and she is surprised while bathing in a pond. From behind some vegetation Actaeon sees her and in turn is seen by Diana. She is angered by the intrusion of the young hunter and converts him into a deer, which is chased by his own dogs.

The myth is specially relevant to the art world because it deals with the sin of curiosity and in general the dangers of seeing, as well as its pleasures. I asked Mr. Droll if I could photograph the place to start planning a video tape. He agreed to that and allowed me into the apartment, where I photographed the bathroom for about 30 minutes.

The tiles around your bathtub can be seen as the vegetation surrounding a pond, while the bathtub, when filled with water, becomes the (indoors) pond itself. After Mr. Droll's sudden death I approached Mr. Rosen [the apartment tenant when Costa wrote this letter. –Ed.] and explained my work in progress to him. He let me into the place and we filmed—at this point with Peter Grass and a small crew of 2—about 30 minutes of raw footage. I have not seen Mr. Rosen since or know of his whereabouts. He is not to benefit in any way from this project and neither him nor Mr. Droll accepted any compensation for allowing me into the apartment.

Once we saw the initial raw footage we realized that we needed more footage and more room around the tub-tiles ensemble. The bathroom is too small to work with our camera and tripod and the screen on the bathtub is another major obstacle to obtaining the right images. At that time we learnt from Mr. Rosen that you would be remodeling the place and therefore we thought it would be best to acquire the bathtub and tiles so that we can reassemble it at another location and do with it as we see fit and for as long as is necessary without having to upset any third parties.

Although our Video is a work in progress and we do not have still a final script, we can assure you that it is meant only for art and educational exhibition. It will be about 20 minutes long and include opinions of some art people on the matter as well as art reproductions of works connected to the myth and very brief acting. Thank you very much for your attention and patience. Please get in touch with Catherine or myself for any further questions you may have.

Sincerely yours,
Eduardo Costa

MEMORIES OF ANA MENDIETA (1988)

First published in "Earth from Cuba, Sand from Varadero: A Tribute to Ana Mendieta," a group of memorial texts edited by Caryl and Clayton Eshleman for Sulfur 22 (1988), 79–82. The title was suggested by Costa for this volume.

I have before me a letter and some postcards that Ana sent to me from different places. Rome, Florence, Malta, Egypt and even New York City. She was always happy when traveling and very affectionate. The cards are thoughtfully chosen and bear extensive reflections on her trips and career, plus greetings. She always calls me "hermano" and sometimes "hermanito."

Ana liked to bring into our conversation intelligent or witty things she would hear around. She was always careful to indicate the source, whether it was someone I knew or not, just as a matter of intellectual honesty (not to take credit for someone else's line). Ana was smiling one day as she told me that she had called Lucy Lippard to inform her that she had got still another grant. What made her smile was that Lucy had said, "Well, aren't you leaving anything for your old age?"

Ana knew how to choose and give a present. Because my wardrobe was quite slim, she showed up one day with a present of clothing. It was a white cotton pair of pants, simply cut, very wearable and appropriate for the summertime. Ana had found the pants in the street, in an area of Soho where she had found clothes for herself before. I tried them on and liked them immediately. They were the right color and texture, and the fit was perfect. When she left I had the feeling that I had been given something wonderful.

The other present Ana gave me is also a found object, although "assisted" by the artist. It is the full shell of a huge horseshoe crab that she found on a Jersey beach. She decorated it preciously with opening and closing Spanish interrogation marks and a number of expertly arranged silver and gold lines which frame the bilingual legend "A chuchazo from Villas, New Jersey." As she explained to me a "chuchazo" is the blow of a whip in colloquial Cuban Spanish, and horseshoe crabs have a tail that reminded her of a whip. She loved the object and understandably so since its natural design, front and back, would make you think right away of some basic patterns in her work. The present was dedicated to me because, before, I had related some of the shapes of her art to different natural formations. I had for instance pointed out a couple of trees on Washington Square which feature natural scars very much like her images in the "Silueta" series. I liked to call them "found Mendietas."

Ana did not like to miss a chance of socializing with her friends. She was a friend of John Perreault whom she also liked to credit with introducing her to the newest art developments through his courses at the University of Iowa. Ana was always glad to meet with him and vice-versa. About three weeks before her death I invited her to dinner, together with Jeff Weinstein and John. Both John and Jeff had visited her in Rome and Ana had proven a good hostess, showing Rome to them, taking them to the right restaurants and so on. We all were looking forward to seeing each other. But Ana was not able to make it to dinner. That same evening her husband was coming to New York and she preferred to stay home with him. Nevertheless she phoned at the last minute to say that she would like to come over just to say hello. Since we were neighbors, she managed to make some time to see us after picking up *The New York Times* for her husband.

Ana did not cook frequently, but when she did it was wonderful. At one point she wanted to meet Scott Burton who had been one of the jurors who gave her the Prix de Rome (another juror was Robert Motherwell and I think there was a third). Scott also wanted to meet her because he, as well as Motherwell, had liked her work very much. Ana asked me to invite Scott to dinner at her place. There she cooked her well-known chiles. Those were an exquisite meal, a simple dish made with very basic ingredients and with a delightful taste. One important aspect: the seeds of the chiles were not removed. When the greenish, perfectly cooked flesh melted in your mouth, the texture and flavor were substantially different (I believe her work, like her chiles, keeps an essential component that most artists discard). Ana and Scott got to know each other that night. Although they did not meet frequently afterwards, at the time of her death Scott called me from England where he was very busy with his show at the Tate. I still have the message he left on my answering machine (I have kept the cassette because Ana's voice is also there). On the tape Scott sounds really upset. "Eduardo," he says, "This is Scott, calling from London. I heard about Ana... How sad... How sad..."

Ana knew a lot of people and liked quite a few of them. Some of these were art people who had been helpful or had charming personalities. She liked for instance Nancy Spero and Leon Golub. She respected them as artists and they had invited her to their place many times since she came to Manhattan. Ana was grateful and glad that Golub was doing well, but worried that Spero would not get enough press or have the right gallery. I think it was after Lucy Lippard's article about Nancy in the *Voice* that her career took off again and Ana was genuinely relieved. She was also concerned that my career seemed to have come to an indefinite halt after a moment of splendor many years ago and I did not seem to care about it.

Ana was small, vibrant and very real. Except for her voice she did not have much physical strength, but she was full of life and plans for the future. Also she knew that her work was going to be extraordinary and the best was still to come. Although critical of our economic system she believed in America's spirit as a force that would survive Capitalism. She believed also that some kind of American dream would come true for her, especially if she was accepted first in Europe.

As an artist Ana was most interesting. Her pieces had a way of illustrating her unusual biography and psyche that was quite extraordinary. Ana was primeval in her approach, techniques and aesthetics when she was working the earth, but she would become contemporary and technological at the time of dealing with the camera and prints. At work she was a prehistoric figure whose playing with nature was recorded many years later by the American tourist in possession of all her gadgets. Her "theme" happens through time, which is a difference between her work and that of the other earth artists. I find this very interesting. There is much food for the mind here. She was in love with the earth and also with laboratories and Minoltas but the nature of these two passions came from a very remote time in history in the first case and from a very recent time in the second case. Probably because her work was about a decade ahead of her time, Ana felt viewers were not understanding her "paintings." She decided then to make her work more available to the established perception of the art world. I would need more space and time than I have to reflect on her changing awareness of the realities of the art world and on the diversity of our dialogue at that time, which helped her find the direction of her most recent pieces.

HÉLIO OITICICA: THE STREET IN A BOTTLE (1994)

First published in Flash Art, *January–February, 1994, 75–77.*

In one of my many informal visits to Hélio Oiticica's second studio in Rio de Janeiro on Avenida Ataulfo de Paiva, he showed me a bottle of shampoo he had been playing with. It was basically a narrow, clear, plastic bottle, and he had removed the label and slid a rubber band onto it, leaving the yellowish contents intact. The rubber band remained in an asymmetrical position, suggesting, he thought, Rio's skyline with morros or abrupt hills. He liked to keep it on the windowsill and to look through it into the street. People and cars would pass by, elongated in curious ways as they crossed the bottle containing the shampoo and the rubber band. Some vehicles were yellow, one was red, a traffic light was blinking. For a while we looked at the show. Oiticica was silent and there was an implicit question in the air: was it worth rescuing as art this moment of random street life seen through this homemade lens? What kind of installation could present this to an art audience?

I have since thought a lot about this work. Oiticica intended it as a simple gesture, easy to reproduce, but it incorporates the street with its objects, people, and cultural contents: the flow of life, the comparison between street and river, the passage of (Heraclitean) meaning in the urban scenario. It also momentarily bottles cars and people and lets them go quickly, a metaphor for the modesty of our vision, its ability to distort the spectacle of life and art, and its fleeting grasp on things. The traveling retrospective[1] of this Brazilian genius (1937–1980) consists of large installations built to Oiticica's specifications, and mostly physically humble pieces that he built himself. Among the most astonishing early works, we should mention the "Monochromatics" (1959), which are one-foot square oils on wood, beautiful examples of painterliness in a minimal format. Oiticica's brushstroke lightly complicates color and texture. The squares are red, orange, yellow, and pink, painted in several translucent layers, and punctuate the wall as did the squares of colored paper Mondrian glued to his New York studio wall in the early forties. Still, this is quite another story. Oiticica's monochromes are hung about one inch from the wall, though parallel to it, and the edges as well as the back are painted the same colors. Oiticica, who left little to the curator's imagination, included instructions: the works should be hung on a white wall and lit so that the paint on the back would throw color on the wall around the piece.

Oiticica had now found his colors, and they remained his favorites until his death some twenty years later. In the "Bilaterals" (oils on wood, 1959) he paints both sides of the support, which is now cut into a shape related to some of the earlier "Metaesquemas," and are painted white. These also come with instructions: they should be presented in a space with white ceiling and walls. In the "Spatial Reliefs" (1959), a large painted plane seems to be folded in an ambitious origami exercise, resulting in free-hanging pieces with numerous angular inflections. Some edges and planes are painted in lighter or more luminous shades of the same yellows, dark oranges, and reds.

From the "Spatial Reliefs," Oiticica jumped into the "Nuclei" (1960). "Nuclei" concentrate the energy of their multi-colored planes in the center, liberating it as they open into space. They exist as either small, non-walk-through pieces or in the larger format of the penetrable nucleus. *Nucleus NC1* is a group of several wood planes that seem to have been folded and then just slightly unfolded. These "unfolding" "Spatial Reliefs" have similar colors, but this time the color is "nuclear," becoming more and more luminous as it radiates from the center. A square mirror on the floor under *NC1* shows a view of the piece's underside. The walk-through *Grand Nucleus* (1964) is determined by several rectangular and square, two-sided paintings. The result is an icon of modernism, the definite extension of painting into space. Basically an enlargement and cut-out of each one of the divisions of the plane in a structuralist painting, measured precisely with an internalized golden rule, the pieces of wood hang from the ceiling forming a "Penetrable." At the time when "happenings," walk-through pieces, audience participation, and other innovations announced for many the death of painting, he pointed a way for it to enter a new domain.

In 1961 Oiticica jumped again, this time toward the synthetic and enlarged format. After trying out each one of the instruments, he now started "playing the music."[2] The *Projeto Cães de Caça* (1961) is composed of five "Penetrables,'" a "buried poem" by critic and poet Ferreira Gullar, and the *Integral Theatre* by Reynaldo Jardim. His own pieces and those by the other artists are brought together in a outdoor "garden" or "labyrinth." Visitors are expected to enter the structure one at a time, and experience it little by little. For Oiticica, the different works, symbolic of their original fields of expression, join another "new and sublime" order. This maquette was a typical example of a piece never built in its intended real size. But Oiticica did not care much about the size of his art. In a way that characterizes the heroic Latin American avant-gardes (even poorer than in Europe or the U.S.) he was able to move on to the next idea with a minimum of material validation (thus the maquette format suited him so well).

"Bólides" followed next. These are visually irresistible, small pieces which introduce the use of volumes of pigment. Begun in 1964, they are mostly jars, boxes, and other containers full of earth, pigment, and colored liquids. Other elements complete the work: a partially painted piece of gauze exiting like vapor from the open container full of pigment, a smaller jar with a different pigment inside a larger one, drawers that open to reveal a mass of color in powder form, and sliding doors that uncover surprising internal areas.

From 1964–1978 Oiticica made a series of "Parangolés." He developed these "capes" as soft "Bólides": fabric compositions to wear and possibly dance within. "Parangolés" incorporate text, pockets with tactile surprises for the hands, and rigid and soft elements activated by the person wearing them. Some of their aesthetics can be traced back to constructivism, but the result synthesizes other sources and is, again, totally original.

Tropicalia (1967) was the first installation built during Oiticica's lifetime. It cannibalized a few of Oiticica's previous works, and the public loved it. It consisted of a walk-through construction of walls made of fabric and other light materials which bring to mind precarious favela architecture, including tropical flora and fauna, in an attempt to stage a "Brazilian state of art." In 1971 Oiticica worked in New York on his "Newyorkaises," of which the penetrable *Nada* (Nothing) seems the most accomplished. The all-black construction features different rooms where light and the projection of the visitor's shadow play an important role. After passing through these, the participant reaches a central room where several microphones are available for discussions about the word "nada" (nothing). It is "an exercise in non-spectacle, non-ritual, and non-significative structure."

The 1973–74 *Cosmococa* installation, a collaboration with filmmaker Neville d'Almeida, provides the most shock value in the current retrospective. It brings Oiticica's involvement with the illegal into the open and dramatizes the role of the artist as an intermediary between the known and the secret, the permitted and the forbidden. In this installation, the floor is covered with sand over which sheets of clear plastic have been spread. The audience is supposed to lie on the plastic, feeling the sand as they hear the sound of Andean music and watch the slide show projected on the ceiling. The images present various arrangements of a white powder on a Jimi Hendrix record, a John Cage book, a Marilyn Monroe book cover, a *New York Times Magazine* Buñuel cover, etc., but essentially surfaces that can be used to form lines for cocaine snorting. The knife as a painter's spatula, cocaine as white pigment, the artist snorting his impermanent work, the documentation of the process and its amplification into spectacle, all validate (artistically) the pursuit of the artificial paradise. It is extraordinary that during the decades of widespread cocaine use in the art world no other artist used the practice as material for art.

In 1978, after six years in New York, Hélio Oiticica returned to Rio with the intention of settling there. A period of exploratory madness, of limit pushing and mega-fantasies, had passed. Back in Rio, Oiticica distrusted drugs, exercised daily, ate well, and had a tan. Having turned forty, his brilliant mind was scanning information gathered over the years, and rearranging it all so that he could establish a steady, prolific flow of work. In his first studio of this period, on Rua Carlos Góis, Oiticica used to work on the floor, his hands busy with the piece, his eyes on the blaring TV set positioned in the same line of vision, somehow still force-feeding his senses.

One of the pieces he continued to work on was a maquette for a penetrable, *Magic Square 3*, of the series "Invention of Color," for which he had done sketches in New York the previous year. In his writings, Oiticica called this piece, with its brilliant yellows, reds, whites, and bits of blue, a "cave of color," and he told me in conversation that he thought of it as a place for people to come in and "take a shower of color." It is important to note that a square, double-sided monochrome

94

painting, and not an architectural notion, is the point of departure. One square painting provided a roof, others acted as walls, a clear square (or non-painting) functioned as "a sun roof," another square painting was a fixed, semi-open door. This painting is particularly important because sunlight can reach the color directly and bounce off onto the visitor. Here color is not something out of a tube, but rather an element for the revelation of light, particularly sunlight.

Hélio Oiticica always talked about the experience of the viewers who would enter one room/painting and emerge into an area unaffected by color, enter another painting and then another, crossing the open areas that bridge them, watching zones of their own skin and clothing assume different colors inside each work. "Maybe I should give each visitor something white for them to wear," he told me, "so that the colors will really show." It is as if he was reluctant to accept the methodical innovation of pure shape and volume that took place beyond the level of mere awareness. The "shower of color" and "tropicalization of geometry" are meant to intensify a subtle, natural phenomenon, revealing it: color does not only impress our sense of vision but also touches the skin, affecting the entire body and astral self as well. Indeed, in the African tradition that so completely informs the Brazilian view and philosophy of life, a certain color is not just an attribute of a deity, but also its manifestation.

NOTES

1. For information on the artist I have relied on artist Luciano Figueiredo, who curated, with Guy Brett, Chris Dercon, Catherine David, and Lygia Pape, the current retrospective, and who designed the accompanying catalogue. Before traveling to the U.S., the show was seen at the Witte de With, the Jeu de Paume, the Tapiès Foundation, and the Gulbenkian Foundation. It will go on to the Guggenheim Soho in March 1995 [The exhibition was never shown at the Guggenheim –Ed.], and the Museu de Arte Moderna in Rio and São Paulo.
2. Esther Emilio Carlos, a Brazilian art critic and the only female impersonated by Hélio Oiticica (in his 1978 performance *Delirium Ambulatorium*), was the first to express the idea that his work was music. Oiticica then adopted the description.

Talking Paintings (1994)

Co-authored with Marta Chilindron. This is the first publication of the introductory text (a typescript that was probably an exhibition proposal) and of the first script "Praise and Insults" (transcribed from a digital recording). "The Hair Jump" and "I Love To Look At Myself..." were first published in Costa/Chilindron *(Galeria de Arte, Instituto Brasil-Estados Unidos: Rio de Janeiro, 1994).*

The *Talking Paintings* are a group of talking wall pieces. This is different from previous works with sound, which feature music, noises, and various poetic texts. Now the sound comes to you as a voice, from the history, the experience, and the feelings of the work. This changes everything. For thousands of years paintings were talked and written about. Now their spirits open up and they speak to us. What they have to say will certainly change the way we look at art.

At the Elga Wimmer Gallery we present the first *Talking Painting* of a series of six we exhibited in Rio de Janeiro in April–May '94. It is a demure work that describes herself in simple terms. If you want more, you can access *I Certainly Do Have A Sexuality,* the second painting in the series, for a bolder speech.

In the whole series we recycled pages from *Vogue, Art in America, Natural History,* and other magazines. That is, we did not use any paint. This just happened, but shows that for us the most important thing about paintings is their format. Anything flat that goes well on a wall is for us basically a painting. The fact that paintings are a successful form is based on their structural characteristics, rather than on paint, or on whatever is painted. Paintings can be transported easily. They can present different universes, and they can be hung on walls. They will be around for as long as buildings have interior walls. Photographs share the same format with paintings, and they are equally successful. Magazine pages may be organized as well to conform to the flat, large shape that can be hang on a wall.

Talking Painting: I Love To Look At Myself...

I love to look at myself for hours every day, alone in this room... facing a mirror that returns and multiplies my image...that reminds me of who I am.

I've finally been installed as I should...but, somebody has to pay the rent, take care of the lighting...and, naturally, people want a payback... So as part of our arrangement I let you look at me... I welcome your curiosity... I even agree to let you come between me and my mirror...let you interrupt my pleasure...

I have to respond to you...as part of our arrangement... When you are around I begin to work...the minute you catch sight of me I adjust to become...everything you've always wanted, in a fraction of a second my trillions of colored dots switch positions...they show you what you love...what you secretly long for...what you fear... I adjust to your whims...that is why I am a good painting...

Right now I show to some of you the laughter of a girl with her first lipstick...to some, the sinister smile of a murderess who just committed her crime...to others, just a fashion shot...and to some I don't show anything...anything at all...

So I am here to serve you, to please you...so enjoy yourselves...but at times I have to focus on my own pleasure...when that happens, you will not be able to see me any more...my voice will fade, my colors, my body...so intense my own contemplation will be...so intense... [Voice fades]

Talking Painting: Praise and Insults (A Diptych)

First Painting:

Beautiful. Thank you. You do look great. I feel like I'm in heaven. Your clothes and, even more, your face, your hair, your eyes. The way you look at things and everybody around you. And your body. Thank you. I do hope I can get to know you better. I love the way you walk and move around, the way your hands move, the fingers, you are so graceful, and you are so attractive, lively. You'll be beautiful and light and graceful always. Wow, what a smile. Just smile at me again, please, stay around. I need your presence. What radiance. I wish I could keep you forever. You certainly have your own light. You glow. You are full of life and love, and I must have done something right to deserve this, meeting you. Thank you, thank you, thank you for coming to this show. I wish you were a performance artist. We could be very successful together. I could just look at you while you dance. Or something. I am glad I am, because I have met you. Perhaps I could make myself smaller, and you can keep me in your pocket. Welcome to this show. You make it all worthwhile. I love your voice, too, your smile, and I am sure I would love the taste in your mouth.

Second Painting:

Hey you there. Hey, sleaze bag. Don't you dare look at me like that or talk to me. Asshole. You better not say a word. Don't think either. You pollute the planet. All of you are such scum. So this is the best you can look, to come to an art show. So what are you looking at? Do you have a problem? Hey, do you have a problem? You're kind of getting old, and fat. Your face is sagging, and your ass too. Gee, you really look like shit. Are you sick or what? Fuck off, scumbag. You know you're a parasite. You look stupid, what a moron, moronic asshole. Get outta here. If I was a man, I'd break your face, smack your fucking kisser against the wall, looking at me like that, moron. Come on, circulate, before I make you eat your shit. Move on, move on, baby face. You look like a rotting turd. And you have dragon breath, too. And you haven't had a shower for a while, have you? Get lost, get lost now. It's the best you can do, believe me. I don't have to take this if I don't want to. Fuck off, you crazy motherfucker.

Talking Painting: The Hair Jump

Psss… Psssst…come here…look at me…come closer please… please, come closer and listen to me.., I guess I should introduce myself… My name is *The Hair Jump*… I am 1.65 meters tall by 1.65 meters wide and 8 cm deep… I was born in Brazil, in 1994…as you can hear, I have a voice… My skin is a new surface, completely plastic, glossy, like wet candy… I am made of many laminated magazine pages, originals from the September '93 issue of the U.S. *Vogue*… These are most of the very few available on earth—as you know people discard magazines right away…my pages reproduce a Roy Lichtenstein painting, *Dorm*, and they were arranged to make: ME…a new entity…

Please don't turn away…keep watching me…keep listening…be patient…will you?…pay attention please… My voice is coming to you through speakers installed in my back… If you want to look at me the right way, you should position yourself some 3 meters away, and I should be in the center of your field of vision… So here I am, self assured and splendid. I hope you will agree, beautiful, intelligent…a lot of people come over to see: ME…partly because I dared to talk… It is nice to have broken a silence of centuries. And now good-bye, good-bye now.

Mestre Didí at Prova do Artista in Salvador, Brazil (1997)

Co-authored with Marco Aurelio Luz. Originally published in Art in America, *July 1997, 101. Courtesy BMP Media Holdings, LLC.*

Deoscóredes Maximiliano dos Santos, known as Mestre Didí (Master Didí) is an 80-year-old Afro-Brazilian artist who recently showed new work in his native city of Salvador. The vigorous insertion of Mestre Didí into the international scene started in the mid-'60s. His work was shown in African museums (in Accra, Dakar, Ibadan, Lagos) as well as at European, Latin American and New York venues. He had a special room in the groundbreaking 1989 show, *Magiciens de la Terre*, at Paris's Centre Pompidou; and he was shown in depth at the São Paulo Bienal last October.

Mestre Didí's works always begin with a systematic unit: a bunch of palm-tree ribs bound together by strips of leather. The sculptures range in height from about 2 to 10 feet, and are enriched by beads and shells. Similar staffs made of leaf veins are used in religious ceremonies among the Yoruba, Mestre Didí's ancestors and his constant source of inspiration. In the traditional religious object, as in Mestre Didí's work, the choice of material is philosophically based: in West African thinking, the ancestors, when they die, go deep into the Earth and come back to the surface as trees and plants. The leaf veins in these sculptures represent the ancestors. A variety of shapes unfold from Mestre Didí's central bunches. The serpent and the bird, associated with the ancestors, are frequent motifs.

The colors of the leather strips that wrap the bunches are post-industrial (the leather Mestre Didí uses is already dyed). However, the colors are never arbitrary or decorative; rather they are selected according to what we can call traditional West African color theory. In this system, the basic colors are white, black and red. Yellow is considered to be a shade of red, while blue and green are shades of black. Colors have certain connotations: in the case of red, action and the flow of life. Large or small, these pieces make us think of Brancusi's work, which itself drew inspiration from traditional African wood carving. The bunch of palm-tree ribs can be seen as an *Endless Column*, suggestive of infinity and representative of the continuum from grandparent to parent to child. Mestre Didi's works have the integrity and the beauty of all great art. When shown alongside the best of today's expression, they easily converse with it, standing out as enchanting and unfiltered contributions to the contemporary. In New York this was apparent in a 1995 group show curated by Arto Lindsay and Diego Cortez at the Luhring Augustine gallery, where Mestre Didi's work was seen along side that of Louise Bourgeois, Joseph Beuys, Matthew Barney, et al.

John Perreault Interviews Eduardo Costa about Volumetric Painting (1999)

First published as "John Perreault Interviews Eduardo Costa" in Judy Collischan, ed., The White Paintings: Eduardo Costa and John Perreault *(New York: Work Space, 1999)*.

John Perreault: How did it come to you to make three-dimensional paintings?
Eduardo Costa: I happened to open a dry jar of paint. The lid had been loose for years. In the inside there was a sort of hard paint-cylinder, separated from the bottom and sides. I saw a new object, a new kind of painting. It was, of course, an abstract painting, which was a pity because it looked like a chunk of dry paint. Wouldn't it be interesting to make a representational painting—for instance, a lemon—on this principle? So I did the first volumetric painting, a representation of a lemon, in 1994. In 1995 I showed several works at the Elga Wimmer Gallery in Soho. A lemon on a saucer, a Chinese cucumber on a napkin, a blue hammer, a bowl with fruit, a black solid-paint demisphere on a blue field, and so on.
Perreault: Why do you present these works as paintings? Can't they be seen as sculpture?
Costa: As a teenager I studied drawing and painting. Then I gave up painting, and at 25 I was doing mass-media pieces. From then on my work was strongly conceptual. I always loved good painting though, and I am delighted to continue the tradition. Also, if I call these works paintings, I am giving a new thought to the history of painting, like Duchamp giving a new thought to an object. I think the part of painting that seemed to be dead is the denial of paint's three-dimensional possibilities. Paint as a material, specially acrylic paint, begs for it.

Perreault: Where does this affect sculpture?
Costa: In this century, sculpture has been made of peanut butter, ice, meat, feces and so on. It's no big deal to add paint to this list. Also, it's time to acknowledge that three dimensionality is not essential to sculpture. It is essential to many of its materials, such as stone, but contemporary art has come up with sculptures that are not three-dimensional. I am sure you will agree that a sheet of paper can be a sculpture.

Perreault: Sure. What differences do you see between painting in two and in three dimensions?
Costa: The problem of light and shadow changes completely. Surprisingly, chiaroscuro is necessary to some extent. In terms of the composition, you can paint different subjects separately, and have them hanging around until you find the right combination. After five years I find new differences all the time.

Perreault: Any special techniques?
Costa: For thin, long things like carrots or bananas, I paint around a slightly oiled wire. I add layers until I reach the body, form and color I want. When the work is ready, I withdraw the wire. For rounder things, I begin with a ball of paint, one of those that painters get when they clean dishes after a day of work. Sometimes I use casts, and then I have to paint the outside of the subject first and add layers until the interior is complete. For flat paintings, I paint on glass, and after it's dry, I peel off the painting.

Perreault: Do you use traditional tools?
Costa: Mostly brushes and spatulas. I also use, at times, the things you buy in art supply stores to thicken paint: marble dust and ground pumice, which painters use to thicken textures.

Perreault: Do you acknowledge any predecessors?
Costa: Tapiès always wanted to come out of the painting with four-or five-inch textures, a mix of sand with pigment. Lucio Fontana somehow made the opposite of what I do, especially in that thing of genius which is just a small canvas with a cut in the center (c. 1950), now on exhibit at Buenos Aires' Museum of Fine Arts. In Brazil, my friend Hélio Oiticica used for the first time pigment in dry form as volume and shape.

Perreault: Since I met you, in 1968, you have done different conceptual works. Now you do paintings. Something to say about this?

Costa: My work aligns the tradition of painting with the conceptual tradition, which is frequently—and initially—part of the tradition of painting anyway. I don't mean "conceptual" in the stupid sense of the frequently boring things done with words. I mean in the broadest sense. The Renaissance was conceptual when it represented three-dimensional space in bi-dimensional paintings or drawings. What a great conceptual adventure! Just imagine, inventing perspective in painting: hence changing the way in which people see reality, so art really animates social perception.

Perreault: What do you mean, "changing the way in which people see reality"?

Costa: I mean that before the Renaissance's vision of perspective became accepted, people saw the sky, for instance, as flat, pretty much as you see it in medieval painting. The stars could be smaller or bigger, but the space did not have depth. The vision of atmospheric depth which we now take for granted, which seems to us the natural way of seeing the sky, is only a few hundred years old. Perhaps it was there before Egyptian, Greek, Roman, and medieval painting, and these great traditions flattened it, which must have been a necessary step. But we don't know that, although I think it's possible.

Perreault: Do you think this kind of conceptual pursuit influences what is painterly in the paintings we see by, for instance, Raphael?

Costa: Sure. The excitement of the conceptual leap kept the artists interested in their own work. The fascination of color or narrative content, the psychological and so on, all great things, can keep up one's enthusiasm only in moments of cultural calm. Then deeper innovation is called in to disturb the peace.

Perreault: What happens to narrative content, symbolism, color, refinement, in three dimensions?

Costa: Once 3D painting is accepted, after the initial frisson, content will become important, and color, proportion, composition and content will matter again. The portraits I am doing are already seen by people as just fine portraits. Nobody thinks, "Oh, gee, this human face is made of solid paint!"

Perreault: You make volumetric paintings, some representational and some abstract. Does this mean you believe these divisions are superfluous?

Costa: Yes. I believe at this point they are.

Perreault: Your squashes are white or green outside and orange inside, and they have white seeds of solid paint inside. You didn't paint them all white *or green, just because we'll see only the outside. This is interesting, because you are expressing yourself in the internal space. A collector who owns one of your pieces can cut through it and see what you did inside. If someone did this, would your work be destroyed?*

Costa: Most of my work gets better if you cut it at least in half, exposing the innards. Even in the abstract pieces something goes on inside—even in the monochromes.

Perreault: Do you think there will be followers?

Costa: I know of two artists who are doing this kind of thing already, and there may be more: 3D painting is a new adventure. Artists will be curious to see what they can do with it. This is not to say that the possibilities of adventure in bi-dimensional painting are over. There is also an infinity in the two dimensions.

Perreault: Do you think your work is of any consequence to art history, and if so, how?

Costa: Well for one thing, after 1994—which is when I started doing "through and through paintings" as Carter Ratcliff has called them—it became technically inappropriate to talk about painting as if it was only flat, bi-dimensional work. It is now possible to describe Picasso as the great bi-dimensional painter of the 20th century, and Pollock as the great bi-dimensional abstract American painter, and so on.

Perreault: In the late 1960s, in the defacto group we had with Scott Burton, Vito Acconci and others, it seemed you had to invent a basic innovation and take it from there: invent your "ism" and then start building your oeuvre on this original foundation. Do you still believe this the best possible thing to do?

Costa: Yes. The average viewer should understand this in time. Scott Burton invented "Usable Art," and Vito Acconci "Body Art," both of them basing their invention in ideas that were floating around in our group. Scott got people all over the world to get to know art with their asses and in public.

Perreault: And white? What does white mean in terms of this exhibition, or in general?

Costa: I am very interested in white outside of painting, as you see it in nature. A white flower, a white egg, the white of burnt bone, eyes or teeth. And, naturally, milk and semen. I think I liked the idea of a white show because we both had white works, and this whiteness is about all that our work has in common. Also, white paintings have been done so much that it may seem the definitive white text has been written. Just to show that nothing is definitive, it's nice to have a different white show. But neither your contribution nor mine is about color.

Perreault: It seems that both of our paintings are paintings about painting—that is, painting as process and painting as substance. And, of course, the history of painting. Yet there are other things. Tell me about those other things.

Costa: Perhaps there is a bit of psychological residue. In my case, personal independence may be a psychological content, since I use only paint and not a support like canvas. So you don't have to necessarily lean on something. Also a kind of promotion of persistence seems to be here, with so many layers of paint.

Perreault: Any projects for the future?

Costa: One project I love is the life-size, volumetric painting of the late Jorge Luis Borges I am working on for the Museum of Fine Arts in Buenos Aires. After giving to painting the three dimensions, I will be exposing it to the elements of the outdoors: sunlight, rain, and the company of birds. Borges' portrait will be a long-term installation in one of the outdoor patios in the museum.

Hélio Oiticica's Cocaine Works and Some Thoughts on Drugs, Sex, Career, and Death (2000)

First published in NYArts *(May 2000), 10-11, with this concluding note: "This text was based on a taped telephone conversation between curator Sergio Bessa and artist Eduardo Costa… It is published in anticipation of the exhibition* Hélio Oiticica: Quasi-Cinemas, *curated by Carlos Basualdo, which will be presented at the Cologne Kunstverein January 2001 and then at The New Museum in NYC, which includes works from the 'Cosmococa' series."*

One day in New York, in '75 or '76, I was doing some shopping to help with lunch at Scott Burton's, and I ran into Hélio on the street. He didn't seem to be well, he looked undernourished and sad, possibly desperate. It was clear that he was doing too much cocaine, and he talked about it. I had memories of him in Rio in 1968, a super intelligent guy in his nice home. In New York City, at least by then, he felt a bit like a ghost of his former self.

He came to lunch with Scott and me, and he and Scott got acquainted easily. Over lunch Hélio somehow came alive. Then he danced for us, demonstrating a certain step in samba dancing which he had told me about before, and that I was trying to explain to Scott. This was a hypnotic, addictive step. People who knew the step had to dance as they heard the music. Their will was controlled by a certain combination of sounds. This step was only taught to the most advanced dancers (Hélio was a "passista" at the Mangueira Samba School, making him something like a general in the army).

It is amazing how the concept of addiction was central to Hélio's thought. Scott was also fascinated by this condition. Even if he would not get into cocaine until the '80s, and he was not into addictive dancing, he had been a pothead for at least a decade and he was certainly familiar with the subject. For these two great artists, addiction, self-destruction, and the fight against them, were a daily exercise.

Hélio was into experimenting in every aspect of his life. That's why, in art, he was on the cutting edge and more, and this is great. To be experimental for too long, however, seems to be a very self-destructive position to put yourself in. I mean, if you want to stay alive, it seems you have to slip into some kind of more ordinary thing. Hélio understood this only to some degree. When he returned to Rio in 1978, he ran every day along the beach in Ipanema, got a tan, ate healthy, and suppressed cocaine. It is a pity that he would break this discipline on extraordinary occasions.

Because I saw him at different stages in his life I can say that he was quite destroyed by New York City's way of life, or perhaps by the way he was not included in it. Even now his work hasn't really been shown in Manhattan. Only a group show in the early '70s—Kynaston McShine's *Information* show at the Museum of Modern Art—and one of the "Cosmococa" works in the mid-'90s. Emotionally he was terribly deprived here. Except for the art activity, there was not much energy, whether human and social or just life energy, he could relate to. Even the landscape didn't give him much. Compared to nature in Rio, this was a gloomy ice kingdom, especially in the winter.

And so he went further and further into drugs. He would tell me, "I shouldn't be doing this, I go without eating for a week or ten days, and I feel great when I'm doing it, I feel I am genius and my work is more important than Picasso's and everybody else's. I know though I am getting weaker and weaker." When he was lucid he realized that he was being destroyed. He didn't realize that the cause was New York, with its particular combination of promise and rejection, its shots of pleasure and its profound loneliness. Not that it was New York's fault, but in this clash of cultures he was left without his support system, mostly family and friends, and he could not replace them with anything else. I believe by now the same happened to Scott Burton, who was not from Rio but Alabama, and to Ana Mendieta, who was from Cuba. It's interesting that these three important artists, not very well known at the time and from very different backgrounds, had met, actually I introduced them, and had lunch or dinner together, and they liked each other. The three died too young (Mendieta at 36, Oiticica at 42 and Burton at 50). Of the three major killers of artists, career is probably the worst. Art making is 95% safe; an art career kills. Sometimes artists are physically killed by anxiety, frustration, the hate compressed in bad reviews, competition, neglect, the fast lane, and so on. Sometimes they die only artistically after they have to face the reality of a career. A career can make a good artist into a dummy, it can empty the artwork of content really quickly. Then drugs or alcohol of course, and sex, more frequently after the advent of AIDS, are the major causes of early death among artists. The three things are interrelated, and combine in fantastically deadly ways.

By the time he left the U.S. to go back to Rio in 1978, Hélio's health was quite bad. I understand he had had two minor strokes, brain episodes where there is a little hemorrhage, but they don't really kill you. The doctors had warned him that he couldn't do cocaine anymore. In 1978, two months after Hélio returned to Rio, I happened to move there as well. I was fleeing the military government in Argentina, and also wanted to avoid New York City or Europe. About a week after settling in, I ran into Hélio in the street, in a most improbable area. After the chance encounter, we remained very close, and met almost daily for more than two years—mostly with a group of artists, musicians and intellectuals that Hélio had shaped and kept alive as a group—until his death in 1980, of a stroke that seems to have been cocaine-related.

In a way he was the typical artist that society puts in the position of experimenting, who can be outrageous, and do all the sexual things and the drug things, even if that means that he or she will self-destruct early in life. This is actually something that happens even more with musicians than with visual artists. People like Jimi Hendrix, or Janis Joplin, or Bird, all very dear to Hélio, are good examples. These artists are the ones society sends out, like explorer ants, looking for new meaning, for more food. The good ones sometimes get to discover this cultural food, but they put themselves at risk, and they may die very early on.

Among the things that destroyed Hélio prematurely were his use of drugs, his not having a steady personal connection with anybody, and, I am thinking lately, his not having a religion or any other strong tradition he could lean on, mostly when there was little or no gratification coming from art activity. Take religion for instance. In his case it could have been the Afro-Brazilian religion, since he was so sympathetic towards Afro-Brazilian culture, and in a way a part of it. Friends that he loved and whose art he respected so much, like Gilberto

Gil and Caetano Veloso, were so openly into it. Since he could not accept religion because of his rationalistic and anarchistic upbringing, he was too vulnerable, even naked.

He had also escaped the world of universities, the bureaus of rational knowledge, the idea that there is in science a solution for human affliction. So he left these cultural shelters for the sake of freedom, of experimentation, and of real life, and found his own enemy which, as it frequently happens, looked like a friend: a drug that gives you a world without pain, that gives you energy any time you want it.

But, and this is most important, Hélio Oiticica did control cocaine as an artist. He did it with the "Cosmococa" series, a collaboration with filmmaker Neville d'Almeida. Hélio once wrote in an article (for the Brazilian *Vogue*) about my first *Fashion Fiction*, that I had "put the famous Marisa Berenson in the role of a model." I should paraphrase him, by saying that he certainly put cocaine in the role of a pigment. Cocaine becomes for Hélio dry pigment, a dry white pigment he uses to draw over record covers and book covers, which were the usual surfaces on which to organize the dust into lines. Because the cocaine lines would disperse so easily, Hélio resorted to photography in order to document his volatile cocaine drawings—and thus the collaboration with Neville d'Almeida, who shot the photographs. This work is very, very important, but it is so important not only because of the far-out, new installation feeling he contributes and how terrific the work looks, but rather the conceptual coup of seeing in this thing that was dominating him, that he could not control, a color—the color white, the last thing an average user would be interested in—and in seeing that he could make some great art with this terrible and seductive thing.

The innovation happened this way: Hélio was doing lines of cocaine on a Jimi Hendrix record cover with the face of the musician on it, and he noticed that he could do other lines with it, lines like in a drawing. Then he made the cocaine lines interact with the image on the record. You see these white lines that look a bit like improbable African scarifications on Jimi or Marilyn Monroe's face. In some of his earlier work—the "Bólides"—he had used pigment as color and form, although he never made lines with pigment in them. It is fantastic that this guy, an artist who was being controlled by cocaine, at one point put a distance, an artistic distance, between himself and cocaine, and controlled the drug with his artistic vision. This is his ultimate freedom, it is his triumph over the drug, and it shows an interesting way out for drug users: you can kick it, and you can use it for something else, it becomes innocuous and even useful if you don't put it inside your body. You just have to put it somewhere else, not in you. You experiment, you acquire the knowledge, then find the place for it, somewhere outside of your body, and keep it there. Not long after doing these works, Hélio gave up cocaine and, in 1978, he moved back to Rio.

It is important to highlight the fact that he made this work with real cocaine as an art material. This is most likely why the whole body of his work has not been shown in Manhattan in a major museum. It was perhaps thought to be improper for a museum where kids would see it. But if these works were ever shown properly in a major museum, like the Guggenheim (which had agreed to present Hélio's retrospective in the early '90s, including some pieces from the "Cosmococa" series, but there was a last minute cancellation via a formulaic excuse) it would be a major event in education through art, and in art history. This work is the triumph of the artist over the drug, and over his own addictive behavior. It is morally and medically very sound work, and it teaches everybody one way to get over addictive behavior. I wonder why work like this is not discussed in art school, even after stories like Jean-Michel Basquiat's or Keith Haring's, or even Warhol's. It would be so good for kids to hear some words of wisdom about the subject.

Some of Hélio's "Bólides" have drawers that are half open, or that you can open to reveal the color yellow, for instance, in all its glory, the real pure color yellow which is pigment in dust form. Some others are or include clear glass jars full of colorful, dry pigment. So, the moment when he sees cocaine as white pigment, and he can use it to advance his work, I have to emphasize, is the moment of freedom, of victory over the drug, and the most creative moment. The artist is enlisting this powerful substance, this addictive demon, as an accessory to his art.

At the time Hélio was making this work, many major artists, including John Cage, were doing cocaine in incredible amounts. There were parties at John Cage's in the late '60s or early '70s attended by everybody in the art world. Scattered around there were bowls with cocaine for all guests to consume. Still the drug didn't show up in any art work done by any of these people. Important artists who were drug users would sever this kind of thing from their art for the sake, perhaps, of their careers. Hélio was very anti-hypocrisy. I can only recall one work (by Al Hansen, which I saw at his place and I don't recall that it was ever exhibited) which made a direct reference to cocaine. It was a small book that had an empty space inside, cut out into the pages, which you could not see when the book was closed. In that rectangular, cut-out space there was a little plastic bag with white dust inside, which I believe was actually talc. The work referred to the well known way of sending cocaine through the mail, inside a book.

Hélio was mostly a painter. His allegiance was to the chain of loosely related artists from cave painters to Giotto to Velázquez to Malevich to Mondrian to Torres García to Marcel Duchamp to Pollock to Beuys (to mention only some names that would pop up in conversation with Hélio) who developed and expressed an "intelligent intelligence" over the millennia. One of the greatest things that Hélio did, was to create this cutting edge work without breaking up with the tradition of painting, or visual representation if you prefer. That is incredible. It is a very Brazilian phenomenon, although Duchamp may have been the teacher. It is Argentinean too, if you think of Lucio Fontana, whose work is the most daring deconstruction of painting (especially the cut canvases without paint, his most radical work).

Scott Burton: The Social Function of Art at the Beginning of the Twenty-First Century (2004)

First published in Ana María Torres, ed., Scott Burton *(Valencia: Institut Valencià d'Art Modern, 2004), 30-35.*

After Scott Burton's death in 1989, I had to go through a large number of his papers, personal belongings, some photographs that he had taken during the period in which he had intended to devote himself to artistic photography and others taken on trips or used for work, family photographs, a couple of important works, and a steel prototype for a chair designed to correct the user's posture. I think about these when I think about Scott, and I also think of all the catalogues, articles written by and about him, interviews, the correspondence maintained with me over the years, and finally all the extraordinary anecdotes and other memories of a close friendship lasting two decades.

Reflecting on this material over the years, I became convinced that there is a central aspect in Scott's thinking that the scholarly professional critics who covered his career only dealt with in passing. Many times, albeit briefly, they have written about his intention of producing an art with an important social content, or rather an important social function. This intention is really the living axis of all his artistic and critical work. This is confirmed by his oeuvre and his testament, a document posterior to most of the critiques about his work and missing from the corresponding biographies. This involves, as far as objects are concerned, continuous interest in both folkloric and industrial applied arts.

In the early seventies, Scott had certain preferences whose fusion he attempts and achieves in Usable Art. These preferences are the aesthetic of the Bauhaus (some of whose members had been artists before working on design, like Rietveld and Mondrian, who with a similar aesthetic produced respectively furniture and extreme painting), Minimalism, Conceptual Art and the socio-political concerns incubated in the nineteen sixties. Usable artworks are furniture and sculptures at the same time, they have a strong conceptual basis, the legacy of Minimalist austerity, and attempt to benefit their users. "I understood [in the late sixties] that it is through work that one should be political or social," is a basic line of Scott's thinking.

Unlike what happened with the Bauhaus and Rietveld, Usable Art is specifically addressed (from museums or in the form of public art) at a socially mixed audience and surpasses the idea of design in favour of more complex objects that steal the functionality of furniture to articulate a series of visual, practical and ideological premises. Usable Art destroys the friendly relationships between the different pieces in the interiors where it is installed. These works, sometimes small and always innocent looking, as in the case of the small end tables made of cement (a material until that time only used for outdoor furniture), or his *Rustic Table* and *Bronze Chair*, make a strong plea in favor of a synthesizing, democratic reconsideration of the history of art and furniture.

The first work of Usable Art that Scott made was *Bronze Chair*, realized at the beginning of the seventies. *Bronze Chair* consists of a bronze replica of a found chair. This found chair had been mass produced in Queen Anne style. It was a product that Scott called *Grand Rapids Queen Anne*, referring to the geographic spot, Grand Rapids, where the factories mass produced reproductions of furniture in the well-known English style in a democratic, non-artisan and anonymous way, and Scott saw the functional, popular merit in this and wanted to perpetuate it in bronze.

Throughout the rest of the decade, Scott experimented with other materials and ideas, producing, among other works, his "Rock Chairs," which I shall mention again below, and in the late seventies he went back to the initial theme, creating *Rustic Table*. *Rustic Table* is a bronze replica of a found table that was mainly made of tree branches. This was part of its beauty. It also had proportions that Scott found remarkable. And, unlike *Bronze Chair*, one might imagine that its author could be a very respectable person, a free, pure artist unrestricted by an official career and identity.

Scott was already negotiating with the market and the art world's structure of power, and would have wanted to be like that artist throughout the transformations demanded by circumstances. By casting in bronze found pieces by an anonymous author, a traditional craftsman, he was paying homage to all authors ignored by the official art system, whose contribution feeds an artistic tradition to which he deeply wished to belong. The proportions of the original, its final form, are the product of the spontaneous projection of a simple spirit that holds the seed of true art and can transmit this seed. Scott could accept official fine arts as his own space as long as he did not have to relinquish the spontaneous arts.

In the last of several trips he made around the interior of the United States, Scott found a stone chair like the one he had made as art on the side of the road. The "rock chair" of Minnesota or Arkansas had been carved out of a roundish rock about 1.5 m diameter by an anonymous craftsman. It had all the basic qualities of a Burton Rock Chair, although the cuts were less precise, the original stone had not been carefully selected, there were no polished parts and rough parts and the proportions were not excellent. Scott was amazed when he showed me the photograph he had taken of it at the beginning of 1989, the year of his death. "The Rock Chairs had already been invented when I started to make mine," he remarked. He was quite shaken by this encounter with the historic truth of his own work.

Suddenly his rock chairs no longer seemed to be original creations, but imitations. Scott knew there were folkloric chairs, tables and benches made with several flat stones, but this rock chair, like his own, was a single piece with a horizontal cut for the seat and a vertical one for the back, which endowed the object with a Minimalist dignity that made it contemporary. Scott thought and spoke about his discovery. The theme was in no way exhausted, but aspects were insinuated that illuminated his role of author of these works that seemed—like *Rustic Table* in relation with twig furniture—to be inserted in a long latent history that was not taught in art school. However, the discovery did not invalidate Scott's contribution but instead clarified it; he was the current, unconscious representative of a pure, profound tradition that he had successfully reformulated in contemporary terms.

Scott's practice soon extended to public art. Like his studio work, it should be usable, socially relevant, open to everyone and perceived as art and/or a pleasant place to sit, a surface to eat on or the place to perform any other useful function. When located in public spaces, the benches and tables that Scott designed for Equitable Plaza and Battery Park in New York, the public park he designed in Baltimore, etc., would be known with the eyes and with the body and used by businessmen, mothers who took their children to play in the park, homeless men and women, the mentally handicapped who happened to wander around the area, and the artistically aware spectator who would understand that, beyond the materials, forms, proportions and colours, these works were the advance guard of a new social art whose features would be established and developed in the 21st century.

In mid-1989, while he was preparing his first European retrospective in Germany,[1] Scott was taken ill and went to the doctors of a United States military detachment in that country. Wrongly diagnosed, he was submitted to an unnecessary operation from which he was never to recover. Shortly afterwards, he was moved to New York in a half comatose state. Scott survived a few more months, dedicating his time mainly to drawing up his will and designing a chair that I shall describe below. His great achievement in these last months was the preparation of this document, in which he ratified his priorities by destining most of his property—a good few million dollars in works, real estate, and cash—to try and have others develop after his death the central theme of his work and writings: the relationship between the fine arts and the applied arts. In the latter, according to Scott, resides pragmatically the problem of the social function of art. The institutional vehicle of this delicate task was to be The Museum of Modern Art in New York, to which he donated his possessions under certain conditions.[2]

Towards the end of 1989, I visited Scott many times. Terminally ill, he found it difficult to speak and did so in a very weak voice. On one of these visits he showed me a chair made of steel sheeting almost one centimeter thick that had just been made according to his directions. Together with his will, it was the project that he had most energetically embarked upon in his last months. He was willing to authorize an unlimited edition of this work, a chair that anyone should be able to afford. So that I could understand it, he asked me to sit on it. It was surprisingly comfortable. You had to make an effort to lean against its back, about 10 cm wide and the same height as your spine, so that it corrected an inappropriate posture and created a beneficial awareness of your body. The seat was made up of two rectangles about 20 by 25 cm, strictly horizontal. The first 25 cm of each user's thighs rested on them. You had to keep far back in the chair so as not to slip forward. I said I thought it was excellent. It was a curative, educational piece of furniture/sculpture. Then Scott asked his nurse to sit on the sculpture to get a woman's opinion. She sat on it and said she felt discomfort below. "Do you mean," Scott asked, "your sexual organs are uncomfortable?" "Yes," the woman replied. Then Scott, too weak to think that maybe he should consult more women or that his chair needed some alteration, said he was very sorry, but the chair did not work and it should not be manufactured.

The history of the fine arts is full of artists whose work criticises or comments on social reality in a broad sense. The phenomenon is manifested in very different ways in Goya and Picasso, Breughel and Hans Haacke, without forgetting Diego Rivera, Lygia Clark and countless lesser known artists. In all of them there is at least one period in which the creative impulse behaves eccentrically, and the artist sees the negative side of social reality and decides, like Buddha, to do something about it. These artists exist alongside others whose art reflects about itself and the medium. Scott's contribution to social art is objectual and theoretical, it provides personal and social benefits for his audience, enhances the value of popular creative traditions and is motivated by what we might call a serious, extreme conviction that led him to try and finance the future venture of his principles and interests when, after his death, others would have to carry on his work.

NOTES

1. *Scott Burton: Sculptures 1980–89*, curated by Jiri Svetska at the Kunstverein für die Rheinlande und Westfalen, Dusseldorf.
2. I quote some meaningful lines from his will: "I give my Residuary Estate to the Museum [of Modern Art, New York] to be held by the Museum in a separate fund to be known as the 'Scott Burton Memorial Fund' for the purpose (the 'Burton Fund Purpose') of publicizing, studying, exploring and furthering the appreciation of the close relationship that exists between the fine and the applied arts, with special consideration to be given to twentieth century work." "From time to time, so much of the net income and/or the principal of the Burton fund as the Director shall determine shall be used to (a) fund the publication of books, catalogs, brochures and other printed materials that further the Burton Fund Purpose; (b) promote and fund exhibitions in furtherance thereof; and (c) provide for acquisitions in furtherance thereof; and (d) otherwise publicize, study and examine the Burton Fund Purpose." "In the event

that the Museum shall decline to accept said principal on condition that the same will be applied for the Burton Fund Purpose upon the terms hereinbefore provided, then, I direct that my Trustee shall pay the same to such other one or more museums or organizations as my trustee shall determine and which shall agree to receive said principal and apply it for the Burton Fund Purpose upon such terms."

Scott Burton and Photography (2004)

*First published as the text for a website created by Costa about Scott Burton's
photographs, www.scottburton.com.ar.*

Scott Burton was born in Eutaw, the county seat of Greene County,
Alabama. Early on, he assigned photography a major role among the
image-producing activities of western culture. In 1987, when he described
his hometown for the Archives of American Art, he did it in terms of
Walker Evans's photographs of that area, a document of the lives of the
sharecroppers of Hale County produced by the federal government's
Farm Security Administration. "It had been one year previously [from
the date of my birth]," he said, "that Walker Evans took all the famous
photographs of [nearby] Hale County and maybe even Greene County,
I can't remember. But that's exactly my area of childhood that was
documented—more the black people than the white. The Coca Cola
signs with bullet holes and the shacks of black people."

In the early 1970s Scott bought a camera, and he commented on
this acquisition in a letter he wrote to me in August 1973. "I have bought
and mastered the simple details of a camera, a 35mm still camera. It is
wonderful to take photographs; I have some vague plan to start to make
photographic objects too, some day," he wrote. His idea was to produce
some art photography, and he started to experiment with out-of-focus
shots. In 1975 he made a photographic work consisting of five black-
and-white frames where I can be easily recognized even as parts of my
face are distorted by the technique. In his own hand he wrote "Portrait of
Eduardo" on the pouch containing the negatives, and gave them to me.

Scott liked very much a cover he made for *Art News* in the mid-
seventies. The cover was a great abstract of Marcel Duchamp portraits,

four consecutive photographs of his own head, which Scott distributed simply on the page. The portraits were Duchamp with the star haircut, Duchamp with his hair full of foamy soap in the shape of two small horns, Duchamp as Rrose Selavy, Duchamp at 85 (taken when he was 58). Scott thought of these as very early examples of art photography, and was happy to have been able to lay them out as the cover of an art magazine.

In conversation Scott frequently mentioned his admiration for several contemporary artists who worked with photography, and expressed his disesteem for others. He admired Cindy Sherman for instance, and also Ana Mendieta, and as a panelist charged with the award, supported Ana's successful candidacy for the coveted Prix de Rome. Scott wanted to meet Ana, and I introduced her to him in the early 1980s, when she was still quite unknown. He also loved the work of classics from Cartier-Bresson to Irving Penn, whose photographs were frequently published in the mass media but commanded, for Scott, full artistic status, surpassing the work of many "art" photographers which he considered slick and banal.

Concerning Scott Burton's Non-art Photographs Included Here

In the late sixties, Scott and I went to a housewarming party in New York's East Village. Scott carried a potted plant as his present, with a handwritten sign that read "this is not an art work." In knowing circulation for five decades, the Duchamp-inspired pronouncement that everything could be art if so designated was itself becoming a commonplace. Everybody at the party loved Scott's contribution. What a relief, something that was not art!

As to what is art and what not, of the roughly 2,000 Burton photographs in existence, I discern the quality of art in around 500. I believe some of these are humble masterpieces of the art of photography, devoid of any technical or esthetic aspiration, yet so naturally tuned to the truth of the subject that they seem masterly to me. Scott never got to complete the "photographic objects" he thought he would create when he bought his first camera, and he never had a show of his photographs. For that matter, he never returned to performance once his reputation as sculptor was firmly established in the marketplace. Even if he considered making another kind of art because he was bored with doing what was expected of him, he had no intention of alienating his established audience and base of collectors by venturing into unknown waters.

These photographs remain as an expression of Scott's pleasure in their taking and as images to be shared with friends. They record his various incursions into the geographic heart of the United States, his vacations in England and Greece, a visit to Switzerland, his weekends in upstate New York or in Long Island's North Fork. In his will, Scott describes in detail his artistic property. He does not mention his photographs in that inventory. That these photographs are not works of art is the conclusion of the knowledgeable people who appraised his material possessions after his death. They were not among the effects auctioned along with his loft on behalf of his estate and the museum that would ultimately be its custodian.

Still, I see art content in a number of them. I see Scott's hand in these recurrent landscapes, in the images of small animals, in the spaces defined by sky and forest, in the individual rocks so full of character, in the bodies of water, in wild flowers, in a few portraits of his few friends. Sometimes it is in the details of architecture and furniture, in the photographs of obelisks, towers, arches, houses, palaces and government buildings taken from unusual angles or under unusual light which brings an uncanny aura to the monuments.

There is no doubt that Scott Burton was ambivalent about the issue of making art available to as many people as possible. Even if he wanted to do so, through his gallery, Max Protetch, he was committed to the production and sale of very limited and expensive editions of his art furniture. In 1987, when he was interviewed for the Archives of American Art, he expressed a synthesis of the dual nature of his ideal and practical positions. "Some of my individual pieces are one-of-a-kind, deluxe objects that only a collector or a museum's specialized support system can tolerate. I can do two or three different things. It's not an ideological consistency. Should I stop doing gallery work if I want to do a production chair? No, I can do them both, and public works."

Interestingly, the fact that Scott Burton's photographs are not officially art puts them in the most advantageous position in terms of the dissemination of the artist's sensibility and vision. These images are free to sidestep the star system with its elitist banality, incarnated in part in the idea of the very limited edition. These non-art photographs, which number comparatively few examples, could be reproduced in editions of hundreds, as long as the negatives are able to originate prints without meaningful detriment of the image.

This site intends to make public the record of a major artist's sensibility at its most relaxed, when free of deadlines, conceptual scripts and market considerations. Given the rigor of framing and the guidance of his own internal editor, we see Scott's mind and eye casually record the greatness of nature, of people and their inventions, and so here they are: my choice of some of Scott Burton's non-art photographs—part of a limited trove of 500 prints and negatives—in their electronic, online immediacy, an introduction to a world that so easily might have slipped away.

How I Acquired Scott Burton's Photographs

After Scott passed away, the bulk of his estate went to his longtime friend, Jon Erlitz. Scott's carefully written will—so thoughtfully crafted that it has become a major source for the understanding of his art and ideas—includes a provision concerning the disposition of his estate. Upon the death of Jon, the estate would pass to the Museum of Modern Art, New York. Ten years later Jon died, and in 2000 Scott's estate went to the museum.

Jon Erlitz gave his friend and roommate of many years, Paul Haug, who also knew Scott, a number of personal possessions and an archive of Scott's personal effects including family photographs, a few of his passports and a prototype for a chair never built. There are also some 2,000 photographs shot by Scott, and a substantial majority of the corresponding negatives. In August 2003 Paul sold this archive to me on the eve of my departure from New York to establish myself in Buenos Aires, returning to the country where I was born. I briefly reviewed the materials, which seemed moving and familiar, and had them shipped to Buenos Aires with my other belongings.

In November of that year the photographs arrived in Buenos Aires, where I could study them with more care. There are photographs of a few friends, their children and pets, some unknown people of interest to him, and many of his favorite furniture pieces. There are photographs of houses, public buildings and monuments that interested him, smart architectural details, the untamed landscape of the Midwest animated by bison and wild goat, mountains and clouds from Switzerland, tiny wild flowers. In them I see Scott's sensibility, his preferences, his keen eye. So much of his vision and character is reflected in these casual images, they couldn't possibly have been taken by anyone else.

Scott Burton's Art

As a young artist, Burton was an integral part of a radical group of New York-based artists that included Vito Acconci, Dan Graham, Marjorie Strider, Hannah Weiner, John Perreault and others, myself among them. Seminal works include his contribution to an anthology for stereophonic tape by artists and poets known as *Tape Poems* (1969), the public performances of "Street Works" (1968, 1969, 1970), "Theater Works" (1968, 1970) and other performance-oriented collaborations. In the 1970s Scott staged "Furniture Landscapes" and "Behavior Tableaux," a series of austere, highly charged events involving furniture, space, bodies and movement were presented at the Wadsworth Atheneum, the Whitney and Guggenheim Museums, Documenta, and elsewhere.

Scott's concept of furniture as sculpture evolved in part from the sets he designed for "behavior tableaux." In 1973 he began to move away from the performative. In a letter to me that same year he writes, "I got $3000—from the government arts endowment [National Endowment for the Arts] and one third is gone in debt, the rest committed to an art work which is not a performance but some objects. These are a table series—useful, that is: functional, but conceived as sculpture, not furniture...an"

Beginning with the casting of *Bronze Chair* (1975), a replica of a found Queen Anne chair, Scott essayed the work for which he is best known, engaging in an open dialogue with the marketplace. As he began to sell his sculpture, these works became increasingly ambitious. Through the 1980s he produced his best-known work, sculpting large, quarried stones and cutting and bending sheets of steel into forms that made them usable as chairs and tables.

Realized as intimate studio pieces or as massive public works, these remarkable objects became Scott's signature expression. These latter works in particular address some of Scott's central concerns. "What is public art?" he writes. "It is, in my definition, art that is not only made for a public place but also has some kind of social function." A 2004 retrospective at the IVAM in Valencia, Spain, and the excellent catalog—Ana María Torres, ed., *Scott Burton* (Valencia: IVAM, 2004)—that accompanied and interpreted the exhibition finally secured Scott's international reputation as the inventor and master of pragmatic sculpture.

THE BIOLOGY OF PAINTING #2: THE ANATOMY LESSON: A DIDACTIC PERFORMANCE (2004/2006)

The introduction was first published on the cover of a 2006 DVD with the same title, documenting a 2004 performance at the Museo Nacional de Bellas Artes (Buenos Aires) whose transcript was translated by Costa for the subtitles.

Introduction:

My "volumetric paintings" (Carter Ratcliff) are created by adding layers over layers of acrylic paint with brush and spatula. Volume is obtained with no materiality other than acrylic pigment and the eventual thickener. The performance documented here was conceived to explain the invisible in my work. My pieces include representational and abstract examples. In representational paintings—fruits, people—I work not only the surface of my subjects but also the internal space. A volumetric painting of a watermelon is green in the surface, white and red inside. A head portrait is as true to the internal organs, muscles, bones—which will be invisible—as to the visible features shown in flat painting or in sculpture.

The geometric abstractions are usually monochromes painted the same color through and through. The knowledge of all the color we do not see conceptually completes the visual perception of the work. I have shown and explained volumetric paintings in Boston, Madrid and Buenos Aires in exhibitions and performances. I have shown them and have taught the needed techniques in New York. Other artists are involved in the practice. I believe the time has come for volumetric painting to integrate established art knowledge.

I am hoping the content of this DVD will change art teaching. Currently acrylic paint is taught as if it were oil based. There is at least one basic difference; utilizing the appropriate techniques, acrylic paint can be employed to build volumes.

The Anatomy Lesson

Here we have a series of works that we've chosen to call paintings, and that this gentleman here whose portrait I have made, Carter Ratcliff, has called "volumetric paintings."

First you see here something like a plate with six eggs on it. If you read the title of the painting, you'll see it's *Half A Dozen Hard Boiled Eggs On A Plate*. The title would tell you that these eggs are cooked, and that what you see is the whites of the eggs. And as it usually happens with represented objects, you would assume there's nothing under the surface except a mass of white paint, that is, if you knew these paintings were made of solid paint only. To show you this painting in full, we are going to cut open one of the eggs. As you can see, with a very sharp knife you can cut one of these paintings. Of course, this is a lot like Lucio Fontana, who once cut a painting. That is, he actually first cut a canvas on a stretcher and showed it as his art, a great work if you ask me. It is in this museum's collection. You can see here how the painting is inside. Can everybody see it?

Audience: Yes, yes

This is a super, ultra representational painting. A super hyperrealistic new kind of representation in painting. Now, the way I would exhibit this work is with both halves of one cut-open egg displayed here next to the plate, or here on the plate. The thing is that anyone who sees this work with the egg cut in half has the right to imagine, yet of course he or she does not know for sure, that the other eggs are similar inside. That is all about this.

Well now comes one of the great moments of this series. This involves cutting a slice of this watermelon. What color do you think the watermelon is inside?

Audience: Red...yellow...pink

Fantastic! We're going to open it as we would do to serve it. We will cut a slice and show it and then leave it next to the whole watermelon because this is one of the most common compositional formats for paintings of watermelons. This requires some effort because really the thing has substance, so the object is resisting. The substance is not the same as with a real watermelon, paint is harder. *Costa and his assistant cut open the watermelon and show it to the audience.*

The next intervention, on the painting of Carter Ratcliff's head, is a little more dramatic because a person is somehow involved. I want to make it clear that the model is a friend of mine—well, I hope we'll still be friends after this! What I am really trying to do today is to put a brain into this head. You see, the internal space is always represented in my work, and in this head there are vertebrae and there's some flesh and jaws and a tongue. What I liked most was the tongue because it came out like something by Picasso. But there is no brain.

And the nice thing about the internal space is that you can sometimes do things you would not do with the outside, you see. It's a fact that we all are very different on the inside and on the surface. Internally the painting is more truculent, and the style it refers to is Expressionism, or perhaps Neo-Expressionism, as there is no three-dimensional version of Expressionism in painting. So on the inside this is a Neo-Neo-Expressionistic painting, and on the outside there is a more simplistic, classical style. Now, Carter is very talented, very intelligent. I am not suggesting that the model needs a brain, it's just that when I completed the portrait I did not make the brain inside, so I will now add it, as a way of paying a debt I feel I owe the model. So we are going to open this head, and take off both the scalp and top of the skull. I don't know if you can see this: the hair is stripes of paint where Carter has written lines of his poems. These are jutting out of his head. This is a collaborative work, and it is actually signed by both of us.

I will read you some verses, "The flesh tries to be all things... "and so does paint. Let's see, another line, "Those of us who lived in the real past." Another one, which has to do with the head, is "You can get new parts for your head now." Well, I don't know how I came to this line, it wasn't planned. But it's exactly what we are going to do now.

OK, here it goes... Don't agonize, don't agonize. This is only fiction...

Audience member: It's a counter lobotomy.

It's a counter lobotomy, as María Marta says. We will add a brain... Let's see, in the meanwhile I will show you...the most truculent moment. The...the blood, if you want to call it that, is fresh paint. There must be blood because we will put the brain inside, inside the cranial cavity, and it will have to stick to the base of the cranium afterward. So the fresh red paint is not just a scenic effect. It has a clear objective, it's functional. That's because as it dries it will adhere—as you know, paint is fundamentally like glue, it will glue almost anything. You could make a chair using paint instead of carpenter's glue, and actually the chair would look very nice if some dripping is allowed. What's going to happen is that between the fresh paint and the base of the cranium there will be a cosubstantiation—the whole thing will become one so that the brain does not rattle inside if you move the head around. Well, it's now coming off. Your attention please... *Costa's assistants remove the back half of the painting, revealing a bloody red interior, into which Costa places the brain. The back half of the painting is then returned to its previous location.*

At the beginning of the twenty-first century there doesn't seem to be any need to maintain the differences between painting styles that we previously had. I am a Hyperrealist painter, I am a Surrealist painter, or I am a Neo-Neo-Expressionist painter and who knows what else. It's more interesting for me to make a summary of everything in my work. The difference between abstract art and representational art did not seem to be so important either. So in some way I took on these styles and made them pass through this whim of mine for making everything out of paint and with volume, to also show that three dimensionality is not only for sculpture.

The next work has three parts, three large triangles. It's the same form, the same triangle in different colors—black, yellow, and white— and various positions. We will show the interior of one of these triangles, how it was built.

What I did here was something like what people do when they use very thin sheets of wood to make plywood, but I used layers and layers of paint. I spread out the paint on a huge table, and once it dried I cut out the form and all parts of the triangle as you would do with plywood, and then to make it stronger I made some ribs of paint that I placed inside, gluing it all together with more paint. So I got an abstract painting, and a monochrome, but a monochrome in which the color is not only in the surface. The color here penetrates through the whole object. You can see how it's made inside. Let's see if we can show you this. Now there is something interesting about these paintings. I don't know why, but if you cut them in half the work is not destroyed, you get two works.

As you may have guessed, the final painting here is an ostrich egg, not a rhea egg, so it's bigger, and we're going to open it to see what's inside: liquid yellow paint. I think it should be exhibited this way, so that the public can see the fresh liquid acrylic paint. Usually only artists get to know fresh acrylic paint, but now this will be shared with visitors to the museum. All these works will be exhibited in the museum's second floor entrance area for three weeks.

The Monochrome in Art and Nature (2011)

First published as "El monocromo en el arte y en la naturaleza" in Blanco sobre blanco: Miradas y lecturas sobre artes visuales *1.1 (September 2011), 62-64.*

Monochromes in art are ineluctably associated with modernity. Monochromes appeared in painting when the canvas started to become interesting as an object in and of itself, independent of representation and its continual references to another reality. The first examples were perhaps the Russian monochromes: Kasimir Malevich (*White on White*, 1918) and Aleksandr Rodchenko (*Triptych of Monochromes*, 1921).

In terms of these well-known examples, we should point out that they are works of a conceptual nature and that they constitute monochromes per se, that is to say paintings—first in oil and later in acrylic as well—that feature just one color, sometimes with variations that include different percentages of white and, on rare occasions, of other colors.

Some recent exhibitions have included monochromes that are not paintings, for example a steel or marble sculpture, but it seems to me not entirely appropriate to include these works. A monochrome finds its fullest meaning when a material (paint, for example) allows us to choose between a wide range of possible colors, and not when just one color exists for a certain material, as is the case with a particular metal, wood or stone.

If it is possible to use several colors in a composition that would show the potentials of a single basic material and we wind up not using them and focus instead on a single color, the viewer can observe a pictoral intention or an extra-pictorial intention in the work. A monochrome can be replete with religious meaning; it can attempt to do nothing more than transmit asceticism; it can bring into painting tendencies from other artistic styles (like Minimalism); it can advance in relation to its own tradition; it can proclaim the triumph of a certain kind of taste (the ordinarily kitsch, the elegantly classical, the austerely minimal, etc.). There are also monochromes that suggest new states of feeling, colors at times beautifully suspended in an as-yet-unexplored zone of morals and taste; these are the ones that particularly captivate artists. Those colors to which no specific meanings can be assigned, but that are pleasing to perceive, or that reveal unknown aspects of the complex and unacknowledged brutal force of color. For example, Russian artists invented the monochrome, but as a continuation and a response to the common tendency within cubism of moving the painting toward a single color (generally, brown, with tones of brownish beige and white).

The origin of the idea of monochrome can be traced to the natural world. There are many many examples of monochromes in nature. Think about white monochromes: doves, white herons and swans, white roses, white jasmines and apple blossoms, white marble, clouds, many types of eggs, milk, snow, and the animals that attempt to conceal themselves in it, like white owls, ermines and polar bears.

Within the monochromes we just mentioned, there are various sub-categories. At the moment, two are of interest to me: monochromes that are completely white—that is, even on the inside—and those whose color is found solely on the surface. White marble, snow, and milk are examples from the previous list of materials where whiteness undoubtedly is an integral element of the entire object. In animals, of course, whiteness conceals a body in which the colors of flesh and blood are found, as well as some white internal elements: teeth, bones, the whites of the eyes.

Milk and semen maintain their color across different animal species, regardless of the animals' external coloration. Women and men can be black or white, and cats can be black or white or several other colors, yet they always have white semen and milk. And blood is always red.

If we think about the colors of other natural monochromes, we can visualize many black birds, snakes, spiders, coal, black stones, beetles, butterflies, and fish. There seems to be an enormous amount of green monochromes, even if we don't limit ourselves to plants, and yet paradoxically it is the most widespread color because of this. There are green birds (parrots are a nice example) and also green herons, though they are very rare, and there are some hummingbirds whose monochrome color mimics the color of the plants that surround it as a form of self-defense.

My contribution to the tradition of monochromes is to have made for the first time what could be considered true monochromes. They are objects made of acrylic paint that maintain the color found on the surface throughout their volume. They are not like monochromes as we know them, a simple layer of paint applied to a structure of canvas, wood, etc. in different colors. For example, my first black cube (made in 1999, each side is approximately 30 cm long, it's now in the collection of Patricia Cisneros in Caracas) was made completely out of layers of acrylic paint and thus maintains its surface color throughout its entire volume. Of course, the perception of this mass of color in my monochromes is not retinal (except for those few cases when, during my didactic performances, I cut through them to expose their interior to the audience's eye). It is not an ocular perception, but it is an imaginary reality that configures a new artistic experience that also has its origin in the simple comprehension of natural monochromes.

After the cubes and wedges whose volume is made up of layers of single-color paint, I made spheres, some strange triangles, rectangles 10 or more centimeters thick, discs (approx. 100 cm in diameter by 10 cm thick), and some other objects that are still thin monochrome paintings but that are separated from the canvas: a pair of dresses, some vases, a pair of small end tables, and, finally, three functional, full-size armchairs weighing 80 kg each. With these extreme pieces, I hope to have set in motion an advance that while somewhat unexpected, is also inspiring to others, and to have invented a new path in the rich tradition of monochromes.

STATEMENT ON FLUIDS AND ART (2015)

Typescript.

The issue of fluids began to interest me in the mid-eighties. For me, semen has a particularly profound meaning as part of an alternative to the Freudian explanation of the psychological origins of painting. According to Freud, what painters create is a symbolization of the child's infantile games with urine and feces. As a painter, I never understood this explanation. Since I had read a lot of Freud and considered him a writer of genius, I was surprised not to be able to agree with this theory at all. I thought that maybe some painters—like Jackson Pollock—might symbolize on the level of the work of art an episode related to what Freud calls the anal stage, anterior to the genital stage in the development of human sexuality. But not all painters. For this reason, it seemed important to me to make paintings with semen, since semen, unlike feces, is not rejected by the body as inassimilable or innutritious; instead, it's one of the supreme creations of the masculine body, a life-giving physical expression. This belief explains my proposal to make paintings with semen instead of paint. That is to say, painting is related for me to the symbolization of the creative fluid par excellence of the masculine body.

And for the female body, milk is the fluid product par excellence. The paintings of milk that I presented, like the *Cube of Milk* and the earlier *Surface of Milk*, now in the collection of Miguel Larreta, are elevated symbolizations and monochromatic representations of the feminine fluid, a giver of life and nutrition.

Bile is a product of the liver, feminine and masculine; it's indispensable for digestion, for incorporating nourishment, for integrating it into the body. Without bile, food would never be completely digested and couldn't be integrated into the blood.

Blood is precisely the fluid that represents animal—and human—dynamism. And it has acquired highly symbolic spiritual meanings in all religions. It has always been indispensable for the sacrifices practiced in almost all the religions before Christianity, which see it as a life-giving force that even nourishes and pleases the gods. In Christianity, blood is of course symbolized in wine.

I wanted to create "a new thought" (Duchamp) for these fluids, new symbolizations. Sometimes, the fluids themselves are present in the work. Other fluids, like saliva, appear in pictorial representations created with techniques and results that are unique and do not exist previously in the history of art. The little painting titled *Surface of Saliva* was made by whipping the paint with very little off-white pigment. Beating the almost pure pictorial medium in this way produces bubbles of air that remain trapped in the acrylic medium. This is one of my contributions to the history of painting. For the first time, the pictorial medium is worked on in such a way that, physically and visually, it represents saliva with remarkable fidelity. The other fluids—blood, bile, milk—were replaced by acrylic paints that represent their color.

DEFINITIONS OF POP ART (2015)

Typescript based on definition of Pop Art solicited by the Dallas Museum of Art for their members' magazine for an article related to the traveling exhibition International Pop.

Pop is a small everyday object magnified many, many times and presented as a sculpture. Pop is a silkscreen print representing the face of a famous movie star left to the imagination of a sophisticated artist. Pop is a large, exactly reproduced, oil and acrylic painting of a crucial frame in a comic strip. Pop is a pretty girl showing off her lovely face and body from all angles. Pop is a professional bodybuilder posing. Pop is an electric chair. Pop is the lonely image of a highway seen sometimes from a moving car. Pop is a flag representing a whole country in the space of a painting. Pop is a gold prop in the shape of an ear of gold reproduced in millions of copies of fashion magazines. Pop is a philosophy disguised as trivia and presented as art. Pop is a brushstroke we used to see in comic strips made into a large size sculpture. Pop is the word LOVE made into a multimedia icon of monumental importance. Pop is a social sculpture in the format of a fashion show made by a group of young artists and poets. There is comic book Pop art, conceptual Pop art, soft porn Pop, "silly" music, etc. Pop is basically a gush of life and energy from the popular mind that reaches all over the globe, mostly between the mid- and late sixties. Pop art seems to require no effort to be understood. Pop is best served by many definitions.

EDITOR'S ACKNOWLEDGMENTS

I would like to thank Eduardo Costa for his support of this project; Clara Tomasini and Pablo Insurralde for their help finding, explaining, and transcribing materials in Costa's archive; Elissa Auther, M.S. Dansey, María José Herrera, Javier Krauel, and Guido Ignatti for our discussions of Costa's work; Jen Hofer and John Pluecker for their translations and for our discussions about translation; and Emmanuel David for his advice and suggestions.

I am also grateful to Marta Chilindron and Marco Aurélio Luz for allowing the publication of the texts that they co-authored with Costa; to Charles Bernstein for permitting the publication of Costa's texts co-written with Hannah Weiner; to Athena Spear for allowing the publication of a 1970 letter from Costa that she had in her personal archive; and to *Art in America*, *Flash Art*, and Clayton Eshleman for granting permission to reprint Costa's articles. I wish I could express my gratitude to the late John Perreault for his permission to republish the texts he wrote together with Costa.

Research for this book was made possible by grants from the Arts and Sciences Fund for Excellence at the University of Colorado Boulder, and the translation was partially sponsored by generous support from the Programa Sur Translation Support Program of the Ministry of Foreign Affairs, International Trade and Worship of the Argentine Republic.

Biographical Note

Eduardo Costa was born in 1940 in Buenos Aires and studied painting and literature, graduating in 1965 from the University of Buenos Aires with an MA equivalent (*profesor en letras*) in literature. In 1960, he co-founded and co-edited the literary journal *Airón*, which published nine issues before folding in 1965. In the early and mid-1960s, Costa published poems and short stories, and he was an active participant in the multimedia experiments in the arts that centered on the Instituto Torcuato Di Tella in Buenos Aires. He lived in New York from 1968 to 1971; Buenos Aires from 1971 to 1978; and Rio de Janeiro from 1978 to 1981. From 1981 to 2003, he lived in New York, where he exhibited his work and wrote for *Art in America*, *Flash Art*, and other magazines. Since 2003, he has lived in Buenos Aires. His work is in the permanent collections of The Museum of Modern Art, the Metropolitan Museum, the Guggenheim, Museu de Arte Moderna do Río de Janeiro, Museo Nacional de Bellas Artes (Buenos Aires), Museo de Arte Moderno de Buenos Aires, and the Fundación Jumex, among others.